IF IT HURTS, IT ISN'T LOVE

Secrets of Successful Relationships

CHUCK SPEZZANO

THE PSYCHOLOGY OF VISION

Arthur James Ltd

I would like to dedicate this book to my daughter, J'aime. She inspired us with her name before she was born and ever after with her living of it.

ISBN 0853053375

Published by Arthur James Ltd
4 Broadway Road
Evesham
Worcestershire WR11 6BH

Cover design: David Kerby Design Ltd
Production: Barbara Cheney
Printed by Guernsey Press

"The whole reason for my work is to make psychology available to everybody at every level in society. I want to put it into everyday language with everyday principles so people will know they have the power and the tools to transform themselves in every situation in every relationship"

– CHUCK SPEZZANO

Acknowledgments

I would like to acknowledge the many clients and participants of my workshops who taught me so much and continue to teach me how little I actually know.

I would like to acknowledge Sam Hazo, poet and mentor for lesson title No. 35 and for the continuing gift of his presence in my life and the world.

I would like to acknowledge Roxi Lewis for her typing and devotion to this book.

I would like to acknowledge Betty Sue Flower, PhD. Her generosity, vision, friendship, and editing skill were the midwifery gifts necessary to birth this book. Without her obvious help I would still be pregnant.

I would like to acknowledge Marcia Crosby for her final editing and concise preparation of this work for publication.

I would also like to thank Jane Corcoran and Susan How for their computer skills in rendering this work into its final version.

I would like to acknowledge my wife, Lency, who has inspired me with love to learn what it means to love. These days a book is really a team effort. I would like to again acknowledge my wife and my children, Christopher and J'aime, for their time donation to this book. And to my friends and readers who helped improve this book with their attention and suggestions.

Finally, I would like to acknowledge the Course in Miracles for its profound effect in my life and healing and its gift to me, my clients and this book.

Introduction

This book is a collection of principles that heal. They are based on what has worked for me personally and as a therapist for over 20 years, and as a marriage counsellor for over 11 years.

Some of these lessons may seem simplistic. I can tell you that they have the simplicity of principles. But I do know these principles work as used. They are some of the principles at the heart of the *Psychology of Vision* that I have been developing since my doctoral dissertation. I have witnessed innumerable transformational and miracle-like experiences in therapeutic situations. I myself at times reach to live these principles time and again as my daily life at times unfolds in problematic ways.

You will notice many of these principles go beyond common wisdom. They are meant to do so. I learned many of these in mind-blowing, jaw-dropping experiences. They represent, in part, my exploration of the subconscious mind. Although there is much more to the mind than this, this is a good start.

This work is unabashedly spiritual. It is what I have found to be essentially part of the human mind and experience whatever name it is called. Whether you believe this book or not – whether you like this book or not – it can still be helpful if you but practice it.

Finally, this book is meant to be a gift – a way of looking at the world in a way that heals pain. I have seen a great deal of emotional pain in my life. Now I understand that most, if not all, pain is absolutely unnecessary. So this is my gift to you – a sincere desire that your life have the love and happiness you deserve.

In many ways this book is a gift of inspiration to me from all the teachers, therapists and people of wisdom and heart who helped me learn and unlearn along the way. This book is a form of heartfelt thanks to them.

1 Intimacy can heal anything.

Whatever assails you in a relationship, whatever brings questions, doubt, or pain – whatever the problem is – the answer will come when you truly move toward your partner. In fact, joining with your partner and recognising a new level of connectedness will heal anything. It can heal all of the deadness, the doubt, the boredom, the fear, the sense of unworthiness, and the emptiness that sometimes come into a relationship. But moving toward your partner does not mean giving up your own position or your own values; it simply means moving toward your partner in love.

Today, take some time and imagine the problem between you and your partner. Now, imagine moving toward them, feeling that you are getting closer and closer. At the point of joining, you have moved past the problems, the deadness, the doubt and the fear. You have reached your partner. If you are having a conflict with, or feel distant from someone, move toward them. You may actually do this physically, or telephone them, or write a letter. Share with them the truth of your own feelings – not to try to change them, but to say, "I won't let this come between us. I want to join you. I value this movement forward, and I value you more than this problem."

Do not let yourself be stopped by anything today. Let joining with your partner or anyone you choose be the answer.

2 Any behaviour that is not love is a call for love.

Today, be aware of all of the different behaviours that the people around you are acting out. Which ones are loving? Which are not? The behaviours that are not loving are really a call for love. And specifically, if there is an attack on you, it is a call for your love. Your willingness to respond to that behaviour – not by defending yourself, but by moving toward the attacker and giving to them – will win you an ally. This person who was attacking, will be very loyal to you in the future, in good times and hard times. But right now, they need your love.

There are some people who are caught in deadness, and others who are caught in attack. Remember how you've felt when you have been in need; remember the cries for help that you have made when you could not even speak the words? In the same way, those who are attacking you are also crying for help, asking for your love. Look around you. Who are you called to respond to? Who are you called to move toward? Who are you called to help?

Think of the person who is attacking you most in your life. Imagine them here with you, and that you move toward them responsively, realising that their attack is the call for your specific help. What is the help that they need from you? How is it that you can assist them? See how you are inspired to respond to them. Are you inspired to call them? To write them? To give something to them? To talk to them?

In assisting them, you will find that these are the very people who have answers for you, if not now, in the future; and if not in some direct way, by being representatives of your own inner experience, so that, in helping them, you help yourself.

3 The beauty of forgiveness is that it changes your perception.

When you see situations differently, they actually are different for you. (Basically, all healing has to do with changing your perception and seeing things in a new light.) Forgiveness releases you from being a victim, from being in a situation you do not like, or from patterns in which you are caught; it allows you to live in a way that raises you above the situation. Thus, the situation changes.

Some people are afraid that forgiveness will lock them into a situation of sacrifice where they will continue to be abused. But forgiveness actually shifts the relationship pattern – it changes you and the other person.

Any area in which you feel stuck, or any place where a person is bothering you is a place that calls for forgiveness. Every problem, every temptation, every distraction, all busyness that is avoidance occurs because we are afraid to change. And guilt hides the place where we are afraid. Forgiveness would move you through the guilt and the fear.

Today, take a look at your life. Look at the scarcity in which you live, at the places where you are in conflict. These are places where you are stuck and afraid to move forward. Look at any illness or injury you have; they hide a situation where you chose not to forgive someone. Now take a moment to dwell on what the illness is. Remember, every situation that seems to be about someone else comes back to an interpersonal level, because all problems are relationship problems.

Once an hour today practice forgiveness in a specific area, relating to a person or situation. Say to yourself, "In this situation, I forgive you, [naming the person], so that I myself am free. In this situation, [naming it], I forgive [the situation] so that I myself am free." With one moment of utter sincerity, saying these words can free you. You are worth this investment of time.

4 Forgiveness is not something you do, it's something that's done through you.

Forgiveness is a choice, an asking on your part to free yourself, to free the situation, and to free those around you. It's something that can only be asked for. Through it, the grace moves through you to transform the situation.

In situations that seem completely beyond you, where you are completely stuck, or in utter pain and despair, ask your Higher Power to bring about forgiveness and to help your unwillingness and your fear. Allow your Higher Power to do all the work for you.

Once in the morning, in the afternoon, and in the evening, sit back and choose a situation that seems chronic to you, that seems utterly beyond your power to change. Take five minutes to think of this situation and to ask your Higher Power to move through you to transform it. Ask for help and forgiveness. Ask that this day be the day of your release.

Then allow the blessing of forgiveness to come through you. This blessing will free you and help you know that everything can be done through the grace of your Higher Power.

5 Freedom and commitment are the same thing.

Commitment is the extent to which you give of yourself in any situation. Yet many people are afraid of it because they think of it as a form of slavery or loss of freedom. Their fear may be a reaction to a lack of freedom they felt as a child, or to relationships in which they gave up being themselves for others' approval. However, those kinds of relationships are bound in fusion; they are a kind of counterfeit commitment that everyone has to face and deal with, which does not lead to freedom.

There are two types of freedom. One is an independent form of freedom, which is a freedom from things, a getting away from things that bother you. The other comes from within. It is a freedom toward, a feeling within yourself that is connected to your level of commitment and your level of giving.

Suppose, for example, that you are in a job where you feel bound, where you are in sacrifice because it is something you have to do. All of the fun and capacity to receive has been taken away because you feel that you have lost your choice. But you always have the power of choice, and can choose to be there, giving yourself fully to your job. Your choice will allow you to transcend your job description or role, to feel the freedom of commitment.

So, in answer to the question, "Is there life after commitment?" the answer is yes! Because what you give creates your freedom. This freedom gives you the space to breathe and to receive in a way that you have not received before. You feel more at peace, and don't have to avoid or run away. Commitment helps you focus on what is important in your life; rather than running away from your life, it helps build your life.

Today you are being asked to commit yourself to someone or to something. You are being asked to make a choice for them because it is your choice that will make them better, and the extent to which their life gets better is the extent to which you will also feel freed. So who is it? Is it a situation in which you are asked to give more of yourself? Is it a person? Whatever or whoever it is, your commitment is your freedom, your freedom is your choice, and your choice will open up the way for you to receive through your giving.

6 The other person in the relationship is on your team.

Your recognition of this allows you to receive from them. They can be the one to save the day and to help you; they have something to give to you, just as you have something to give to them.

Do you act as if the people in relationship to you – especially those closest to you – are on your team? Do you realise that they are part of your movement forward in life, that they increase your ability to win? Have you recognised that as they succeed, so will you? Have you been treating them like strangers? Have you been acting as if they've been the enemy? Have you been fighting over who's going to get their needs met first? If they are losing or failing in some way, it isn't by accident. You have been competing with them as if they were on the other team to show them and the world that you are better.

In the morning, choose someone who is close to you in your family or at work, whom you have considered to be on the other team. Today, all day, begin to act toward them as if they are on your team. Start with your thinking, then with your feeling, and then with your behaviour, and act toward them as if they are on your team.

This evening choose somebody that you truly love – your partner or someone who's close to you – and think of them as on your team, too. Their winning is your winning, their success is your success. Give them your support. Let your creativity emerge as you think of ways to support the persons closest to you.

7 Your partner is not here to meet your needs.

Often, at the beginning of a relationship, we experience a glow like the relationship is made in Heaven, that we've found a person who is going to meet all our needs! Of course, when they don't, we decide this is a relationship from hell.

One of the greatest mistakes we make is to think that our partner is here to take care of us, to be our sugar-daddy, our great mama. But, expecting your partner to meet your needs will actually hold back the relationship because eventually we resent anyone we think we need to meet our needs, whether they meet them or not. Any time you have a bad feeling, you will think it is their fault. Any time one of your needs are not met, you will think they need to go into sacrifice to take care of you. There will be no way for your partner to win.

But this is not the purpose of a relationship. The purpose is to make you happy, and your happiness comes from your ability to make contact, to give and receive.

If you feel that you are not happy today, take a look at your attitude toward your partner. If you feel they have been put here to meet your needs, be willing to change your attitude. Be willing to move past this mistake, to make another choice. Be willing to see that your partner is here to co-create with you, to make contact with you, to communicate with you, to help you move forward together and to heal with you, arm-in-arm, until you become fully happy.

8 The more you control your partner, the duller they get.

When we first start a relationship, we are greatly attracted to our partner. They thrill and excite us. But as we move on in the relationship, things that excited us become the very things that threaten us. So we try to control our partner, to shut down the very area that attracted them to us; we want them to share that only with us and not with anybody else. But of course, it doesn't work that way. When you shut down attractiveness in any area, it begins to shut down all over. If you are successful in controlling your partner to make them safe, it also makes them duller, and thus you create your own boredom.

Your willingness to give up your control, and let your partner be attractive will stir up the fear you have inside, that little area where you feel threatened. Be willing to experience this because it will bring back the excitement. If it gets too fearful, you can communicate about it, which can create healing. But don't try to shut your partner down.

Today, begin to lift the controls that you've had on your partner. It may be time to communicate about your fear that you might lose them, this area where you have been frightened of the gift that they have. Communicate with your partner about how much you value and appreciate their gift. Take off the control. Take off this form of blackmail, and just let them be who they are and fully enjoy them.

9 You can only feel rejected when you are trying to take something.

You can only feel heartbroken or rejected when you surreptitiously take from your partner under the guise of giving. It's like getting your hand slapped as it sneaks toward the cookie jar. So when you feel hurt, rejected, or heartbroken, ask yourself, "Where in the situation am I giving to take?"

Wholeness makes no demands. No one can reject you when there is nothing that you need. In moving forward, fully giving, you cannot be pushed away because you are irresistible. It doesn't matter what the other person's behaviour is because you are not trying to have them do it your way to meet your needs. What you want is just to love through giving, which nobody can stop or reject.

Your exercise for today is to let go of what you have been trying to take, and to give fully, to give your support without asking that anything be returned to you ... and you can give to someone thousands of miles away. Giving is not a form of manipulation or a sacrifice to get something back from someone. When you truly give, it will move you forward, open you, enlarge you, and enhance you. Through it you will truly receive and enjoy the fruits of your own giving – love itself.

10 To recognise bonding is to have love, forgiveness, and bliss.

Bonding is the natural state of things. So when we recognise it, we are not recreating it, but realising what is already there. When we move through the illusion of separation, we experience a sense of connection, and through it we feel energised and supported, we feel the Source within. Conversely, by holding on to the misperception of separation, we lose an opportunity for healing, and create a place of even greater pain and seeming separation.

One form of healing is simply to go back to the perception of pain and reconnect with everyone. And as we move through misperception to recognise the bonding, and to experience connection, we experience love and the giving forth which is forgiveness.

Look at where you have seen distance, and see the real connections. You may have been looking only at the places of separation. Now, look beyond that for the things you share with people, look for places where you are connected with people, and where you feel as one. As soon as you recognise one place where you feel connected, you will begin to see others.

Today, where there is a problem in a situation, think about what you share with others so you can begin to realise your connectedness, the healing, the love, and the bliss. Then you can begin to enjoy the abundance.

11 A broken heart is always an attempt to control someone through guilt.

It means that you are on the losing end of a power struggle. Basically, your broken heart is an attempt to make the other person feel guilty so that they will meet your needs or do things your way; it's a form of emotional blackmail. This attempt to control will not bring you happiness, and it will not get your needs met. It will just create a bigger power struggle.

Today, be willing to move toward, instead of away from your partner. Be willing not to use your feeling as a bludgeon to get your partner to do what you want them to do. Instead of fighting with your partner and using different forms of manipulation, give them a gift. This may be a physical gift or an emotional gift, as long as it is something you freely and fully give to them. If someone has broken up with you, an external gift may be a form of manipulation, and refused as such. So if this has happened to you, give them an internal gift, such as forgiveness, letting go, gratitude, or sending them love without attachment. The extent of the gift that you give will be the extent of your release.

12 Under every defence is a place of old pain where we are still trying to defend ourselves.

The problem is that although the defence doesn't always block the pain, it always blocks out the good things.

It is time now to be willing to experience the pain under the defence, to have courage about this feeling, and to recognise that it is an illusion. Today, look for a place where you or someone else is defensive. Where they are defensive, there is pain and need. If you ask yourself what they need and respond to it, you will find them willing to let go of their defensiveness to move toward you.

Within yourself, find the feelings you are hiding by looking for places where you run away or attack – the two favourite forms of defence. Now, take some courage, and be willing to feel your feelings, to move through your old pain until it is over. Remember, no feeling is bigger than you are. Now, be willing to feel what is underneath those feelings until you get to a place of peace. Once you do that, you will be freed of having to carry around all this extra armour. You will find that the energy from the defence is given to you, as well as the energy from the feelings that have been hidden beneath your defences. This will put you back in the flow so that, once again, you can receive.

13 You control because you cannot stand it being so good.

All of our control operates as a means of self-protection. But control only protects and perfects our fear of getting hurt, which covers up the fear that if we let go of control, things would get really great, and we would be overwhelmed. It would get so good that we would just go into "meltdown" and be totally lost, so good that all purpose would be gone and we would die. But guess what? This is only your ego scaring you with death. If you gave up control, you would not die; only your ego would – and then you would feel like you died and went to Heaven.

Take a look at your life. What is the control situation staring you in the face? Do not forget that we are capable of using others by having them control us. The bottom line is: we arrange to prevent feelings so overwhelmingly good because we think we cannot stand them – yet, this is largely unrecognised. Give up control, and a giant reward will come to you. Today is a day for you to receive in a big way.

14 To have what you want in a relationship, keep seeing and feeling what you want.

Our ability to imagine or see, feel, and even to hear what we want in a relationship creates the fact. Our mind is a great creator. Often in relationships, when healing is taking place, we experience side effects that we do not wish, and things seemingly get worse. But if we keep in mind the healing we want, and allow ourselves to feel and see it, we can help realise what we want more quickly and easily. By doing this, we remember what our goal and the truth is – if it does not contain true greatness, it's not the truth.

Today, your goal is to feel and see what you want in your relationship. What would be happening? Feel it, and let it go. See it, and let it go. Hold no attachment to what you envision, but know you are programming your mind; this is helping you to manifest and create the very situation that you want. Do not be afraid if things seem to get worse at first. Healing is simply taking place, and hidden poisons are coming to the surface. As they do, keep the vision you have for your relationship, and share it if at all possible. This will help you move from where you are, to the healing point.

Nothing can stop the power of your mind. Nothing can stop the truth, which has to do with joy and happiness and love.

15 When you wish to have a need fulfilled, give the thing you feel you need.

All pain comes out of what we feel we need and the fear that our needs will not be met. In other words, we're afraid of what we'll lose or what we feel is missing; so instead of accepting our fear, we push it back and resist it, which generates pain. The more we do not accept our fear, the more it hurts; the greater our resistance, the greater our level of pain and fear.

In some situations, the need may be a little bit more hidden. For instance, you may feel like you need more sex and that you are willing to give sex at any moment, day or night. But what you may be called to give is not the act itself, but more sexual energy. This higher level of giving would create the very thing that you are needing right now.

Today, be willing to look a little deeper into your needs. What do you need? Give it to whomever you need it from, without imposing your giving on them. Give the feeling of your greatest need, give the energy of it to them. If you have a general need, give it in general. If you feel you have a specific need from a specific person, then give it in the same way.

The need to dominate comes from fear.

Whenever we are in a situation where we are trying to dominate, or someone is trying to dominate us, there is probably a frightened child inside the one dominating. So when someone is trying to dominate you, think of how you would respond if there was a child near you who was afraid. Respond to that need. Be reassuring and supportive and you won't end up feeling like you are oppressed.

If you are trying to dominate someone, there is a part of you that is feeling frightened. What if you communicated your fear? Communication, reaching out and forgiveness can heal the fear, and would be a great gift for the other person.

Today, in every situation that shows itself in domination, reach out, communicate, and forgive.

17 In any conflict, both people are acting in opposite ways, but feeling the same thing.

Knowing this is the beginning of creating resolution, and the key to healing any conflict: while the two of you may be acting in different ways, the point of joining is a feeling you have in common. For instance, the feeling of fear can create fight or flight; or guilt can create withdrawal or aggression. In both cases, the reactions stem from a common or shared feeling. If communication begins with your feelings, you can create a mood of sharing where both of you have one point to agree on. From this point of joining or agreement, the whole situation begins to unfold in understanding and joining with the other person. Whatever you are experiencing, you can use it as the barometer for what they are experiencing, even though their behaviour may be exactly opposite to yours.

Today, be aware of the people with whom you are in conflict. Take some time to dwell on what you are feeling in this situation, and be willing to send the other person whatever you believe would heal the feeling that you share. Be willing to bless them.

18 Blessing is the antidote to sacrifice.

When we are in situations of sacrifice, we feel unworthy; we do not feel good enough to be equal in the situation. So, we feel we have to give up who we are, and only do things for others.

Blessing is the opposite of sacrifice; it is your desire that things be good for the other person and the situation. Blessing says, "I have power. I can give in this situation. I don't need to sacrifice myself. I can give forth a blessing, which will make the situation better." By giving your energy, love, and best wishes that things be good, you change the situation in which you felt as if you had given yourself up.

Today, dispense blessings to everyone, especially in situations where you are tempted to judge someone. Release your judgements, release all temptations to go into sacrifice, and bless everyone with whom you come into contact.

19 **Bonding is our true reality.**

We live in a world of illusion in which we all seem separated. But we are like islands in the sea. If the sea were removed, we would find one firmament, one land. In much the same way, all of us experience ourselves as separate, and yet in the deepest area of the mind, there is only one mind – the Mind of Love. Everyone who has reached enlightenment has experienced that all the world is one. Everyone who has had glimpses of Heaven realises that unity, union, and oneness are all truth of higher consciousness. That is why connecting and moving aside the illusion of separation is the healing of the world.

This morning, take a moment to close your eyes. Imagine yourself as a little baby in your mother's arms, with your father and your whole family looking down at you. Allow yourself to feel how much they love you, how grateful they feel for your presence. Maybe there are things missing, like money or a nice home, but you are here, and they feel grateful for that. They feel connected to you and love for you. Let go of any feelings of separateness, and just feel how much they love you and want you.

In the evening, imagine that you are being held in the arms of God. Let go of all your cares and worries, everything that has been on your mind, and let yourself be held like a little baby. Feel the connection of love between God and you. You can feel that force surrounding you, the love moving through you out into the entire world, creating a network of connection, a network of light. Feel yourself at home. There is nothing to do, and no place to go. There is just you, the child, receiving all that love.

20 When you join another in their place of isolation, they heal, and you receive a gift.

When people around you have withdrawn inward and isolated themselves because the experiences of life have been so painful, recognise that they need you. In fact, any problem of life is a result of this withdrawal. Find that cave within them where they have hidden, and stand outside, pouring your love toward them, smiling because you love them enough to see where they've hidden themselves.

As you join them, your love will move them through and into healing. It will get them moving forward once again. As they move forward, responding to how much you've cared for them, they will come out of their isolation, their illness, their pain, and you will also receive a gift.

There is one person today that you are called upon to reach out to, a person who has withdrawn. Let them come to your mind, and even before you begin to move toward them physically in any way, move toward them in your mind's eye. See yourself joining with them. Your caring, love, and responsiveness will make a world of difference to them – and to you.

21 Creativity will fulfil all your needs.

Needs give us tunnel vision. They make us think that we lack something, which can only be fulfilled through a certain situation. So we limit our response, or fulfilment or resolution in all situations. In contrast, creativity comes from our love for someone or many people. It provides us with a way of looking at the world or any situation from an expansive viewpoint.

Some creative project or new thing is calling you today, something that would unlock you and release you from your need. What is this creative act or project? What is this form of creativity that would release you and give to you and to the whole planet? Creativity is your gift of love to the world. Who are you giving this gift to today?

22 In the river of a relationship the important thing is the bridge, not the banks.

Many times in a relationship we feel that if we moved and surrendered to our partner, the point that we wanted to make would be lost. But if we build a bridge to our partner, our point would actually get embodied and integrated with them. What is important then, is not to fight for our side of the bank, but to build a bridge to our partner. As soon as you do this, both of you will feel as if you have been heard, and responded to. Both will feel satisfied, because the new form integrates the truth of both the banks, creating a form of intercourse between you.

Think of someone from whom you feel some distance, and imagine that you are building a bridge from your bank across the chasm. As the bridge reaches the other bank, feel them coming to join you, and feel yourself going to meet them. Feel the energy from their side coming to meet you, and the energy from your side going to meet them. Feel how good it is. Notice the results as commerce begins for both of you, and how it changes the existing situation. When you build a bridge, you get both banks, which are part of the same river.

23 What you reject in your parents, you will act out.

The way we have judged our parents is, deep down, the way we have judged ourselves. So we react in one of two ways. By rejecting a behaviour in our parents, we act it out as a way to understand what drove them to that behaviour in the first place; or, we behave in a totally opposite way as a compensation for how our parents acted. We form roles out of our judgements against our parents – roles that lead us into sacrifice with our children or our partners. And ironically, we are stuck with what we have rejected in our parents.

Take a look at what you have rejected about your parents, and see if you are acting in the same way, or a compensatory way. See if you are acting out a role that makes you do good things, but does not let you receive (this eventually leads to burn-out). Your understanding of their situation, and your willingness to forgive them will release you both. Allow God's Love to help you forgive them, and say from your heart,

> In God's Love I forgive you, Mum.
> In God's Love I forgive you, Dad.

24 If you have a grievance with another, apologise to them as if you were the one causing it.

The remarkable thing about grievances is that we feel really right about every one of them – so right that we get stuck in them, and do not move forward. We make certain people play certain parts to justify our anger and attack. Unfortunately, we do this so that we can hold onto a belief system that is hurting us. It is almost as if, hating gorillas, we locked ourselves in a cage with one.

Under every grievance is guilt. So when you have a grievance, you project what you feel guilty about on to someone else. The most powerful way to find the truth of this secret is to apologise for what you thought they were doing to you. Suddenly, you will realise that it was you who was doing it. You will feel the emotion come back, and an understanding of what you had hidden from yourself.

Today, reflect on what you are getting to be right about and let it go. List three people with whom you have grievances, and see them, write them, or call them. Apologise to them for what you thought they were doing to you. You will find your release in your apology.

25 If you are exhausted, you are playing a role.

Many of us get thrown into exhausting situations in which we burn out. But we cannot burn out unless we are acting out our beliefs about how we should be. When we act out of our roles, rules, and duties, we may be doing things that are unnecessary, or to avoid certain feelings, or to keep ourselves from receiving good things. We are doing the right things for the wrong reason, out of habit instead of choice.

Choice energises us. To change a role into a place of energy, choose to do what you are doing, rather than doing it because you are supposed to. When you feel most exhausted, set small goals for yourself. Each time you reach a little goal, you will gain more energy. Be willing to do the right thing for the right reason.

Look at a place where you feel exhausted. Imagine now that this exhausted self is really some kind of mask or costume. Remove the mask and see whom you find underneath. You may find a person from your family, a monster, a little child, or maybe even yourself, in need of support and dealing with some painful feeling. Ask how you can help them and respond to that need. Imagine holding them or yourself, supporting yourself, coaching yourself.

26 When you are feeling dependent and needy, let go and trust.

The scariest thing to imagine when you are feeling this way is to let go of what you feel you need. Yet, this is exactly what would bring success, because when you give up your attachment, you move into another level of attractiveness and partnership. Every time you let go, you take the relationship forward to a new level of joining and romance. But the more dependent you become, the more unattractive you become. You begin to seem more like a burden to your partner. It is as if you are pushing them away while trying to grab them.

If you really value your partnership, be willing to let go. Do not get in your own way by your dependency, which is a form of trying to take without being able to receive. Trust that as you stand empty-handed, something even better will come to take its place. Once you do not need it, it can be given, and you can finally receive.

Imagine giving all of what you need into the hands of God and let your Higher Mind decide whether you need it, and what you will receive. Expect good things to come your way. Your willingness to trust will allow you to move forward.

27 What you resist in another will persist until you accept it.

Any time you have a problem with someone, or a situation persists, it is because you have a lesson to learn. When you accept what you are resisting, you will forgive the other person, and move to join them. But the more you move away, the more you will be stuck in the situation because the resistance is still there, holding you back.

Imagine the person you are resisting the most. Feel yourself moving across the intervening space between you and them. Feel the light within you moving to join the light within them. When you feel both your lights joined, allow yourself to sit in that peace. During the day, check to see if that sense of peace is still there. If the peace has been disturbed, it may mean that you are going on to another layer of the resistance, so take the time to feel yourself moving again to join with their light until, once again, you have reached a place of total peace.

28 Abundance is the result of willingness to receive.

All of us say that we desire certain things which we do not have. But if you were to know what is in your deeper mind, you would realise that what you lack, you do not want because for some reason you are afraid to have it. And the more you complain about not having it, the more you are actually afraid of having it. Check out your belief systems and fear level. You may be kidding yourself about what you say you want. For example, your belief system may say, a good person should not be rich, or abundant, or have so much sexual satisfaction – or whatever you think you need but are not receiving.

Look within, and know the problem is not the situation around you or the person near you. It is you. Be willing to change your attitude, to have courage and open yourself up to a new level, to find your hidden fears, and to look at your belief systems. Somewhere you have valued an idea or a certain feeling (maybe guilt, maybe fear) more than what you think you want.

Today, let the negative beliefs that stop you from what you want come to your mind. Let go of whatever belief or feeling stands in the way of your receiving. Imagine yourself just being filled with what you want.

29 It is not the truth unless everyone wins.

In any form of competition or power struggle where there are "winners" and "losers", it is only a matter of time before the "loser" strikes back. The only situations that truly work are those where both people or parties get to win. This situation is not built on a false economy, but on a movement of energy into a higher form. Both sides in a power struggle have some of the energy (if not the form) of truth. Joined together in integrity, they bring an integration of all perspectives in a new vision – which is what truth is. So, settle for nothing less than everyone feeling as if they have won. Do not stop the communication or the negotiation, and accept no compromise. If you do, everyone will feel as if they have lost, and as if they are in sacrifice.

Your exercise for today is to be committed to the people who oppose you until both of you can get to a point of feeling as if you have reached a new resolution, a new vision – a place where everyone wins.

30

Pain is an area where we have cut the lines of relatedness, where we have removed ourselves, or pulled back from someone.

Maybe we didn't like what someone was doing, or maybe a situation seemed too difficult to overcome, so we decided not to recognise the relationship. Instead, we cut ourselves off. Years later we suffer as we allow ourselves to get in touch with places where we have cut the threads of connection with old friends and family members, or even parts of ourselves.

Today, see who comes to your mind as someone with whom you are called to reconnect. Reach out to them and extend yourself so you can remove the pain you are experiencing, consciously or subconsciously. Just feel the connection with all of those people, and reach out to them.

31 Sex is communication, not just the plumbing, or being a good pipe fitter.

What are you communicating to your love partner? Whatever you communicate is what you get to experience. If your experience in sex is just a form of release, of getting your needs met, then you are keeping sex very small. If your energy around sex is that it is just something you were told not to do – it will have the excitement of forbidden fruit. But if you do not go past the taboo, and the feeling of excitement that comes from it, you will be limiting sex to its first stage.

Sex is a powerful way of making contact and communicating. And communication is one of the great healers. Sex is one way of moving through power struggles and reaching out to your partner. It moves you forward through differences to create a new sense of reality, of partnership, and release. Both communication and sex can heal, it can move you out of feelings of deadness – if it is more than just the physical experience. The very essence of sex is communication, it is the emotional and the spiritual – it is all of the joining and contact that you can make, all of the getting to know who it is that you are really making love to. As you are making love, you get to receive from and give to your partner fully. You get to enjoy them totally.

Look at what you have been communicating to your lover. Maybe you have withdrawn from sex. What is the message you are giving to the world – and to God? Be willing to reach out once again, to open the door to sex, to move forward to a whole new level. Do not make love, let love make you.

To heal boredom, take an emotional risk.

Are you tired? Feeling down and out? Feeling dead? Feeling like you cannot be bothered with your partner because they are *so* boring? Yet, our boredom, like all our other emotions, is directly related to us. So, what are you withholding? How are you holding yourself back in the situation? What risk are you afraid to take? What are you afraid to communicate?

Communicating about what we have been afraid to reveal will create excitement and a new emotional energy for us. If we communicate about the things we are afraid would destroy the relationship, we will discover that not doing so actually has held us back from each other and has begun to destroy the relationship. To heal boredom, be willing to take that emotional risk, to work through whatever is necessary, to take responsibility for your own experience, and to move forward toward your partner.

Let come to your mind what you have been holding back. That is what you are to communicate today. Do not stop communicating until both of you feel that you have been heard, until you both feel you have won, until you both feel peace, and until both of you feel you are moving ahead together.

33 In any relationship, one person will be the problem-finder and the other will be the problem-solver.

In any relationship, people will polarise into two positions, both of which serve the relationship, and enable it to move forward.

One person will seem more pessimistic, though they'll call themselves realistic. They will be good at communication, more in touch with their feelings, and highly discriminating. Their chief gift is to find the problems or possible problems in the relationship. The other person will take on a more positive role, and be more of an idealist. They'll be more diplomatic in their communication, where the problem finder or "negative" will be more out front. Though somewhat naive, the "positive" will be able to transform situations.

While the "positive" will sometimes blithely commit way beyond themselves, the "negative" will know exactly how much energy, money, and time something will take. Working together, positives and negatives make a great team for success. If the positive and the negative both realise that the other serves a vital function in the relationship, then the two can move forward as a team. The negative can get in touch with the problems, and the positive can transform them.

Take a look at your major relationship. Are you the problem-finder or the problem solver? Are you appreciating the job that the other person is doing for you? If you learn to value your partner, you can really move forward today. Give them appreciation for the function they are serving in the relationship. Learn to value their input, because it is through them that you both move forward.

34 Giving is receiving.

Giving is one of the best feelings in life, and is to be distinguished from sacrifice, which does not allow you to receive. When you are giving, you are truly feeling your greatness. All that you give automatically opens the door for you to feel good and to receive in that moment. In fact, many of the early tribes were so generous because giving allowed them to feel their greatness of spirit.

The extent to which you give to a person is the extent to which you feel them giving love to you. So if you are not giving you will not feel open enough to receive – even if they are totally giving you love. In giving, you recognise what has been within you all the time. Every time you give a gift, you get to experience it, and as you do, you receive back the very gift or feeling that you are giving – you give, experience and receive your greatness of spirit.

Today your task is to imagine you have all the resources in the world, and you can bless people with whatever it is you think they need. Throughout the day, take the time to give to certain people. Go beyond yourself. Support those around you. Give a little bit more. Smile a little bit more. Reach out a little bit more. Let one person come to your mind who you will give a special gift to for no good reason except that it is your joy.

35 **"Expect nothing, and anything seems like everything. Expect anything, and everything seems nothing."**

—Sam Hazo

Anything can create wonder and provide new ways of thinking, whereas expectations are limiting. If you have a picture of how it should be, your expectation will lead to disappointment and frustration. Your willingness to let go of all of your expectations, to let go of your pictures of how a situation or someone should be allows you to move forward. Every expectation is a demand of someone else. When you feel demanded of, how do you react? Sometimes you may just totally refuse, or sometimes you may give what is demanded of you. But if you do not enjoy giving, it may make you feel oppressed.

Today, notice one area of frustration and disappointment in your life. Be willing to let go of how you think it should be. Be willing to let it go so you can move forward into wonder and new ways of thinking.

36 The extent of your expectations is the degree of your stress.

Stress typically stems from "busyness" in your life. Where you have a large number of expectations, you are working very hard with very little reward because you cannot receive. That is because expectations have to do with the should's, have-to's, got-to's, need-to's, ought-to's, and must's rob us of receiving. Expectations are also demands which come out of a feeling of inadequacy and "neediness". So we try to take care of these needs by controlling outward situations or ourselves – imposing the same expectations or demands that we make on ourselves on everyone else. Yet, the closer we get to an expectation, the more resistance we feel against finishing. In contrast, the closer we get to a goal, the more it attracts us naturally.

Today, look at areas where you feel pressure and stress. You may find an expectation of yourself or of the situation that is holding you back. Letting go of it is a way of letting go of the stress.

Consider all of the unfinished projects you have. Let go of the ones that are no longer timely for you. Reset your goals for the others, and take one step forward after another. Do the same thing in a relationship by setting small goals of healing and of having things be better. Move into the flow of life and surrender to it without trying to make things happen. Your trying to make it happen creates stress and blocks you from receiving.

37 Expectations are time bombs waiting to go off.

The more you expect, the less you receive. This is because expectations are your picture of what will make you happy. But happiness is not something you can demand from a situation. You can, however, generate it from within or receive it.

Expectations are a way of covering your hidden needs while you pretend that this "neediness" (this inadequacy) has nothing to do with you, but has everything to do with your partner. When you are in an expectation mode with your partner, you either make banal, small-talk, or you make demands. The latter, of course, creates resistance and naturally leads to power struggle. As the resistance builds, it is only a matter of time before there is some sort of explosion or separation.

However, your willingness to let go of your expectations can give you expectancy. Expectancy is a positive feeling, a knowing that what is coming is the best thing for you, even though you do not know what it is. Let go of your expectations or demands in favour of this positive expectancy which allows all good things to come to you. Invite. Do not expect. Know that the best is coming your way.

Today, get in touch with areas in which you are not receiving and where you have a certain sense of urgency. These are typically areas where you have expectations. Be willing to let go of your expectations and trust that what is coming to you will move you forward.

38 Expectations ruin experiences because they place a demand on the situation to meet your needs.

So even if the situation lives up to your picture of how it should be, there is a good chance your needs will not be met. At the same time, this is a way of ritually killing all the inspiration of the event. Expectations are different to goals, which are good to have because they invite you forward and are much more productive and successful. If you move toward a goal and miss it, you simply re-set it. But if you miss an expectation, you beat yourself up and make yourself feel bad, which does not facilitate moving forward.

Be aware of your expectations and willingly let go of how you think it should be, so as to be taught by the universe about what is the best way for you. Trust that, at the very deepest level, everything works out for the best for your healing and growth. If you are willing to accept this, to let an experience be anything and all that it is, and make full contact in any situation, you will have a much greater chance for happiness.

If you have an event coming up where you might have expectations, imagine the event as a city at the end of a beautiful, emerald river. Imagine getting into a little boat, and launching it into this gentle river. As you move out into the current in the boat, you can just relax and watch the scenery go by. The river itself carries you toward the city, to your goal, and it feels so easy. There is no effort necessary. As your goal calls you, there is nothing to do – just relax and enjoy. Repeat this exercise whenever any worry or stress appears. Use this until you reach your goal.

39 What you repress, your children will act out.

Sometimes as children we experience certain events that are traumatic or painful. So we fracture off the parts of ourselves we thought got us into trouble and repress them. (Any area of failure is typically an area where you have repressed something.) In repressing them, we forget about them, and then we forget we forgot them. But what we have repressed will then show up in the people around us as we project our lost selves on to them. This is especially true of our children. For example, if you have repressed a part of your sexuality, your child may seem very precocious sexually. If you have rejected a part of yourself you considered dishonest, your child will always seem to be lying.

You cannot divorce your kids, so you are always being motivated to work through whatever issues your children seem to have, to understand and accept them. Our children act out for us so we will finally have a chance of forgiving those lost parts of ourselves that we have believed got us into trouble, and thus release our hidden guilt. Through our forgiveness, we integrate for our growth and healing those parts that have shown up in our children. As you learn to get back in touch with your feelings and to re-associate with yourself, your child will be released also.

Pick a problem your child might have. If you do not have children, pick someone very close to you. Choose a quality you dislike intensely in them. Imagine that you are drifting back through time and space to the point where you pushed away this particular quality. How old were you? Who was there during this event? What was occurring then that you judged this part of yourself as bad and wrong? Now, reach out to that little child who doesn't understand why you are pushing him or her away. Take her into your lap and hold her. Nurture and give to him, and then, feel him melting into you and disappearing. When integration occurs, whatever is negative falls away, and the energy will be subsumed into the movement forward in growth.

40 The more you love yourself, the more you can recognise that you are loved.

And yet, one of the greatest problems in the world is that most of us feel unloved. If you are not loving yourself, you are giving everybody the message, "I'm not worth loving" – which puts people off. Even as our family and friends love us, we can easily not experience it if we do not feel any love for ourselves. If you are not recognising yourself, no one else will.

Do something today that is an act of love for yourself. Start by taking a close look at yourself. Where can you respect yourself more? ... and give yourself credit? ... and recognise yourself? ... and really reach out to yourself? What could you do that would be a gift to yourself? Not as an act of indulgence, because indulgence doesn't make you feel loved (it actually wears you out as much as sacrifice does).

Many of us are much harder on ourselves than we are on the people around us. Today is the day to give yourself a break, and to recognise how much you deserve. If feelings of unworthiness or valuelessness come out today, just feel them until they are gone. Don't turn away from them or try to cover them up. The simplest act of healing is to be willing to feel your feelings until they evaporate. Underneath, you may find even more loathsome feelings. Through this process you will find an opening through which to receive others' love and to feel your own love for yourself.

41 **Temptation occurs when a new level is about to be reached.**

It is a distraction that we use to delay ourselves from moving forward, which is our personal conspiracy against our greatness. Such a delay only serves our fear – even when it is the fear of having it all.

When we have personal connections there is typically a sexual attraction too. Many times when we feel these kinds of energies, we run or jump in to indulge ourselves. But if you refuse a temptation, you allow yourself to move forward. By bringing your energy back to the relationship, the quality that you were tempted with will develop in your relationship within the next two weeks. Your willingness to keep that particular energy flowing toward your primary relationship will make it stronger and more whole.

Sometimes when we refuse to yield to a temptation on a physical level, our mind will keep lingering on a particular quality that the other person has that would somehow, we think, meet our needs. But the ego serves that temptation up to us when the need is just about to be met in the primary relationship. If we take the temptation, our mind is split, and our time is wasted by moving in two directions at once. Problems and pain are bound to ensue.

All connection with others is really a creative energy or project that is there for both people. If you indulge yourself without discernment, often the guilt or problems that ensue will cause you to lose the connection. If you move forward with integrity when you get to a certain closeness, a love energy will emerge that makes all of the sexual energy safe.

Today, look closely at what you are being tempted by. Be willing to move that energy toward your primary relationship, because as you do, that relationship will be able to unfold and give you new gifts, even the very quality of the gift with which you are tempted.

42 Staying open and feeling your feelings creates healing.

Many times when we are attacked, whether or not it has any vestige of truth in it, painful feelings arise – guilt, anger, fear, hurt, frustration. When we are confronted with attack and the feelings that ensue, we often run away, dissociate, or attack the person back. But the best response is to stand defenceless and as open as possible, so you can feel all the feelings as they come up for you. Just feel them until they have melted away. They are neither right nor wrong. They are simply true because you are experiencing them. They don't necessarily have any outward truth other than that. Take whatever time you need. In the end, there is peace and happiness. Just be willing to feel, knowing that as you finish, you have completed a step for both the attacker and you, and the relationship will move forward.

Today stand as defenceless as possible and take courage in experiencing your feelings. This by itself can be the healing that moves your relationship forward.

43 The less you expect, the more you receive.

Your expectation covers up a demand, which in turn covers up a need. Your need has a sense of urgency, and whatever you feel you have to have creates resistance. So the very thing you are trying to get, you are secretly pushing away. The more you feel you need it, the more you create resistance to being able to receive. The more demands you place on the people who might give it to you, the more likely they are to pull away – even if it was something they wanted to give to you. It takes a person of great maturity not to move away when someone expects something of them. Once you let go of the urgency, you provide the opportunity for your partner or the people around you to willingly move in to fill the gap, to respond and give to you.

So who is it that you have major expectations of today, and what do you have expectations about? Get out of your own way and let people give to you.

44 The independent partner can move the relationship forward by valuing the dependent partner.

Many independent people who are committed to their relationship do not realise that they have the power to transform it. If you are the independent person in your relationship, learn to value your dependent partner because they serve a vital function. Be grateful that they handle all of the pain and "neediness" in the relationship. To reach them, you have to reach through your resistance to your own neediness. As you value them for this, you bring them up to your level, and the relationship moves into a new level of partnership. This also raises them up to a new level of attractiveness whereby you both win.

After you have reached this new place and celebrated it, the relationship will move on. You may be, once again, in the independent mode and your partner the dependent one. Just reach out and back for them once again and pull them up to you. Each time you do, some of their neediness and your hidden neediness will be healed and the relationship will move forward.

Today, look for someone who is needy around you, and willingly reach out to them and raise them up to a new level of confidence by valuing them, and to a new level of feeling good by appreciating them.

45 To have an exciting relationship, take an emotional risk.

If you feel you are stuck in a rut, that you are in the same old pattern in sex, communication, or how you live, then the antidote is to take an emotional risk. If things have become this dull and boring, you are withholding some vital energies, some vital communication. What don't you want to tell your partner that you feel would hurt them, or that would destroy the relationship? Communicating about these things can bring new life back to your relationship. The intention is not to wound your partner but to share with your partner, to say, "This has held me back from you, and I don't want it to keep holding me back. I take responsibility for this feeling. This is not your fault, but I am willing to experience it fully and share with you so we can make it better together." Sometimes saying this will trigger a very painful response in your partner. At that point, move forward and genuinely support them. As you reassure them, you will find your relationship has moved to a new level.

As you share these things and get them out of the way between you and your partner, there is a chance for new growth, and for the realisation of a new connection to emerge. If you value the relationship, be willing to take the risk that keeps the excitement generating. Be willing to deal with what is not working so you can make your relationship better.

Today, take the emotional risk that would make things better. Who is it you have been hiding from? Who is it you have been afraid to share with? Remember, you can say anything to anyone if you are close to them. If you are standing in great intimacy with anyone, they can receive anything. They know your intention is to move forward in commitment, rather than to make them wrong or to pull away from them.

Perception is projection.

Whatever you see is a reflection of what is in your own mind. In other words, the way in which we see the people around us reflects our belief systems. If we change them, we take away the limits we place on others to be all that we are. And when we take responsibility for what we are experiencing as the movie of our mind, we have power in the situation. For example, if you did not like a particular movie, you would not try to change the image on the screen. You would go to the projection room and change the film. The film is like our belief systems, and the projection room is our own mind. What kind of movie are you making in your life? A tragedy? A comedy? A love story? An adventure? Or is it a movie that even you would be too bored to watch? What could you do to change your perceptions? ... to make a decision about the kind of movie your life is? But what changes any perception you may have, no matter how complex, is forgiveness, and your willingness to see where you chose a certain event.

If you had a major experience in your life, whether positive or traumatic, you may have decided certain things (created belief systems) about life or about people. Sometimes, totally contradictory belief systems will sit side by side in our mind, so that, at different times one belief system or the other will be at work. What makes this situation even more complex is that the one at work may be a belief system we have kept hidden from ourselves; and so it may be difficult at first for us to locate or identify what film we are playing.

Take a look at your partner. What do you have to believe about them for them to be the way they are? Your willingness to change this belief and to see a higher value or belief will begin to change your perception of them. Deciding to examine and change your subconscious beliefs will change the film you are projecting onto the screen of your life. When you realise that everything you see and experience is your responsibility, you can become aware of what you are doing in your projection room, and you can make better choices for a happier life and a happier relationship.

47 When you give and get hurt, you are giving to take.

Many of us have the attitude that we have given the best years of our life to old what's-their-name. We feel we have wasted our lives, or that at times when we have given, we have not been recognised and have come away hurt and rejected. But the only time you can be hurt when you are giving is if you are giving to take – you put a contract on the person to give something back in the way you desire.

If you give freely, you cannot be pushed away because there is nothing you are trying to get. If you need nothing, you cannot be rejected. If you are giving just for the sake of your pure love, there can be no hurt response. When you give out of your fullness, you get to receive fully, and it does not matter what the response is because your giving is the full reward.

Choose someone to whom you have given in order to get something back in return, and give something to them freely. Give something you feel called to give, something that would release you from the whole entanglement. Let go of any expectation or demand for a particular response, knowing your giving is your reward.

Guilt always hides fear.

Guilt is a place where you have made a monument to a mistake and left the path of life to worship there. Guilt withdraws you and withholds you from the people you love. You may feel you have made a mistake in relation to your partner and feel guilty about it; but consider, not only does guilt reinforce the mistake, it starves your partner of the very love and nurturing they need. Your willingness to allow the next step to emerge will cut through fear in much the same way that forgiveness cuts through guilt.

Look at how you have used your guilt, or your bad feelings, to hold yourself back because you have been afraid of the future. Look at how you have been living because you have been afraid the future will be the same as the past. As you release your guilt, the future will reveal a greater horizon and call you forward to it. You have no need to be afraid of your future.

Today, make a choice to no longer be held hostage by a mistake you have turned into self-punishment. Making life all about yourself through guilt is to make yourself unhappy. Choose to learn the lesson involved rather than to arrogantly belittle yourself and make life all about you – when it is really all about happiness or the healing to bring happiness about.

49 What bothers us, never bothers us for the reason we think.

Typically, we are so out of touch with ourselves when we are upset that we never realise what we are upset about. We often confuse ourselves, diffuse what we are feeling, dissimulate, and present to ourselves different rationalisations about what is going on.

What you are upset about can be coming from a much deeper level – from the subconscious or the unconscious mind. So when you are upset in a relationship, look again. What you are feeling may be just a trigger to get you in touch with feelings you have carried for a very long time. You just needed a trigger in the present to get the old pain out to be healed. If you are really in touch with yourself as you feel any sort of pain, you will recognise how much of it is coming from past situations. Almost all pain is coming from the past. As you communicate about where that original pain is coming from, you can begin to heal your natural self-expression and communication.

Today, begin to communicate about at least one event that is bothering you. Share it without any attempt to change the other person. As you finish sharing what it is that is bothering you, reach into yourself and feel the feelings under your complaint. Share these. Then, reach deeper and deeper into yourself to all the feelings you can experience. Sometimes you may even find a situation coming to your mind where these feelings began. Stay with the feeling. The more you share, the more you free yourself from this old pain.

Receiving is giving.

In fact it is one of the greatest forms of giving because the more we receive the more we just naturally pass on our abundance to everyone around us. Our willingness to receive is a real gift. Many people love to give, but they have a very hard time receiving, and are, therefore, thrown into sacrifice instead.

In partnership, we have a real fear of receiving until we reach interdependence. When we learn to receive, our very receiving makes the people around us feel loved. When your child offers you a little weed as if it were the most beautiful flower in the world, their giving with heartfelt love transforms the weed into a beautiful gift. And your willingness to receive the transformative power of their love is also a gift to your child.

Today your exercise is to be willing to give to your partner and to everyone around you by just enjoying them and receiving whatever they give to you. Accept what is being given to you and realise how much more you are being given than you normally receive. Take a look at the sunset, and everything that life is giving you as it comes your way. Today is a day to fully receive and enjoy yourself.

51 What you are expecting of another, you are not giving to yourself.

If you were to love and recognise yourself, you would open the door for other people to love you. Stop complaining about what other people are not giving you, and give it to yourself. Then you will find that many people not only have the ability, but the willingness to give to you.

Take a close look at what you've been complaining about not been receiving. Today is the day to start giving it to yourself. Every hour, on the hour, give whatever it is you have been wanting. Remember, it is not necessarily the form of the thing, such as sex, money, and so on. It is the energy of the form.

52 Dependence is trying to get needs met in the present that were not met in the past.

When dependence tries to take in order to get old needs met, because they are old needs they can never quite be filled in the present situation. It is an attempt that will always be unsuccessful. Only a realisation of this and forgiveness will release the past. You can move forward out of dependence by letting go of the past and letting go of those needs in the present.

Take a look at the person you might be seeking approval from, the person you might feel dependent on. Who was it, really, that you were trying to get love from? Imagine yourself as that little child who did not get love, and then give to that parent or person the very thing you thought you needed from them.

53 Any problem is a fear of taking the next step.

If you are willing to take the next step in a relationship, the problem can disappear, or it may just turn into something to be handled – but it is no big deal. A problem is just the part of your mind that you are not giving. For instance, if you are giving seventy-five percent of yourself, then twenty-five percent will show up in problems that seem to be thwarting you. But what is between those two pieces of your mind is fear. Your willingness to move forward and take the next step transcends the fear, allows for the integration of those two parts of your mind, and allows for the problem to disappear.

If you think back, you will realise that any time you have truly taken the next step, no matter how big the problem was, life always got better for you. This time is no different. Be willing to move forward. It is the easiest way to remove yourself from the most complicated problems.

54 If your relationship is stuck, you are afraid of what would happen if it got unstuck.

And wherever it is stuck is an area in which you have been afraid to receive. You have controlled this area and hidden it away, and possibly blamed your partner for not giving to you in this area. But where you are not receiving, you are actually afraid to receive.

Look at where you feel stuck and what you might be afraid of receiving. What would happen if this part of your relationship was unstuck? What self-image and what behaviour would you have to give up? What feelings would no longer be true for you to carry around? Ask yourself, "What is the purpose of my not receiving this?" Are you afraid that if you did receive, you could not trust yourself? Are you afraid you would be overwhelmed by how good it would be? Are you afraid you would not trust your own integrity?

You are at the heart of this conspiracy. So you have the power to transform any area in the relationship. You could become unstuck by your willingness to give up control. Do it today.

55 Your pain means you are making a mistake.

As a child if we stuck our fingers into the fire, we would pull them back and learn not to do that again. But emotionally, we have stuck every appendage into the proverbial fire, and we still have not learned the lesson – that something needs attention. The thermometer to let us know we are somehow making a mistake is pain. If we paid attention to it, we could begin to heal.

Today is a day to learn that wisdom does not come from suffering. Wisdom comes from learning the lesson that heals the suffering. Realise you have made a mistake and you can heal yourself if you move past what you are experiencing. Open yourself up. Spend ten minutes today in meditation about any particular area of pain, and ask your Higher Mind for help in understanding the lesson. Be willing to learn it. Ask to be shown the way.

56 We try to control only when we have lost confidence and trust.

Control is a response to our fear that we will be hurt as we were before. In the subconscious, under the need to control, there is always old heartbreak, which is a place where we have lost faith and trust.

Trust is the power of our mind, when all of its parts are joined together focused in one direction. Bringing our trust into a situation creates confidence, which will allow us to let go of control so things can move forward. If we were to trust, even those things that look tragic or negative would begin to work for us because of the very power of our mind.

Today, in any situation, take a look at what you are trying to control. Bring trust to this situation, beginning with yourself. Because all problems come from a lack of confidence, your willingness to trust yourself and the people around you to do the very best means everything will work for you. Trust is not naiveté but using the power of your mind to unfold a situation.

57 Our experience and memories are perceptions, not events.

Our personal beliefs and attitudes are the filters through which we see things. In any situation, we are really experiencing the filters through which an event unfolds – not the event itself. And further, as the event becomes a memory, we will remember it differently as we move through our lives. So an event that is shared by two persons, then, will be experienced and remembered differently by each person.

At different moments in time, we make up stories about our past based on facts that fit our present mode of operating in the world. As we grow and change, our attitude toward the past changes, and then the way we remember and experience it changes. In fact, we have very little idea of what, for example, our childhood was actually like. As we heal ourselves, many times our opinions about our mother or father or siblings are transformed. When we come to a full understanding of any event, including all subconscious elements, we realise no one is to blame, not even us. The hurt in the situation falls away because truth has to do with a level of understanding that releases all pain. All healing has to do with changing our perceptions into something more true. We know it is the truth because there is no pain connected with it.

Today, in any situation where you may be experiencing conflict or pain, begin to communicate. Most misunderstandings and misperceptions are healed as a result of clarification. Use communication as a vehicle to clarify any misunderstandings and misperceptions, and to experience the other person's perception of the event. This will bring both of you to full understanding.

58 When your partner opposes you, you are called to a new way of life.

Realise, in a relationship, two people form one mind. So your partner brings forth aspects of the truth that are very important, both for your growth as a couple, and for you as an individual.

When they have an idea or an answer that seems exactly opposite to yours and may even seem to threaten you, life is just telling you it is time to move forward, to learn from their way of doing it, and to find a way that is best for both of you in a higher form. When you have integrated both ways, you will have reached a new level of partnership, and you both will have a higher level of confidence and be better able to receive.

Today, appreciate what your partner brings to your relationship. Even though your partner may be acting different from you, your own growth and life vitality are connected to your willingness to change and integrate what they have to give you. As you grow together, your differences will provide more flexibility, a wider perspective, and a new level of partnership and success for both of you.

59 When your partner is polarised from you, integration will take you to a new level.

All healing at some level has to do with integrating parts of yourselves you have lost. When your partner is polarised from you, they are expressing something you are being called to integrate, which will take you to a higher level of partnership. When you integrate an opposite, you do not get any of its negative aspects, only its power and energy. The integration will show itself in the highest possible form, and it will contain the energy of both of you so you both feel you have succeeded.

Imagine you are actually holding a miniature of your partner and yourself in each of your hands, with each of you representing a part of the truth. Now take the pictures you have in your hands, and melt them down to their pure energy, so you are just holding two hands full of energy and light – the most basic building block of the Universe. Notice there is no difference between the energy in one hand and the energy in the other. Now bring the energy together, so as they are joined; you will see a new image, a new symbol, a new form begin to emerge out of all that energy. Allow that new form to come into your life, joining you and your partner.

60 You can feel rejected only when you are the one pushing away.

If your partner is acting in a certain way in order to get needs met, and you reject their behaviour, you are the one that will feel rejected. In fact, when anyone rejects a person, situation or experience, they are the ones who will feel hurt.

Notice that you are in charge of your feeling of being hurt, of your rejection and heartbreak, because you are the one pushing away. If you are willing to move toward your partner, whatever the circumstance, and take your judgement away, to communicate and just to give to them, this feeling of hurt will disappear.

Today, avoid the temptation to reject. In areas where you feel hurt, move toward the other and give to them without any form of expectation. You may have suffered a disillusionment. But getting rid of an illusion is always helpful if not a happy experience, because an illusion cannot sustain you. You may be resisting the loss of certain dreams. And it may become clear to you that it is time to make new decisions based on the situation, but it can be done without having to resist or reject the other; rejecting the person, situation or experience, will create a dark lesson for you. The beliefs of this event, which come from the decisions you make, can start or reinforce a painful pattern.

You are in charge of your feelings. Nobody else has hurt you. Transform all your feelings of rejection into positive feelings of giving no matter how your partner or anyone else is acting.

61 The other person in your power struggle has the missing piece you need to make yourself complete.

A power struggle is an opportunity to win back a lost piece of yourself. The piece that was lost is represented by the person who opposes you. When you move toward this person and quit judging them, you can join them in such a way that they are helped. After you have reached out and opened the door for them to come through, you will receive from them the vital missing piece that can bring you to a whole new level of growth.

Imagine your supposed enemy standing before you, representing a part of you that has been lost. As they stand before you, pull off the enemy mask and costume and see the part of you that has been lost. When you do, ask yourself, "How can I help you?" Reach out, support and love, and hold that part of you so as to win it back. As you give to that part of you, if it is a child, as the child is supported and acknowledged, he or she will begin to grow and mature right up to your present age, and then just melt back into you.

62 **Loneliness comes from proving you are special.**

As we separate ourselves, we become lonely. We do this because there is a certain poignancy to loneliness; as we suffer quietly by ourselves we get to feel the pangs of our specialness. So we choose loneliness because we would rather be special than make contact with those around us. But specialness always leads to pain. It is always a form of separation, of looking for special kinds of needs to be met. Not one of us is lonely unless deep within ourselves we want to be.

See that your loneliness comes out of wanting to be different. You are asking to be treated as special, and yet you are afraid of your essence and uniqueness, which is a leadership gift. Today you are being asked to let go of this veil of specialness, this veil that will keep creating pain for you. Give up your choice of loneliness and make contact with those around you. When you move past your need for specialness, you will find that you are recognised and appreciated, and that you have a natural attractiveness.

63 When you are afraid to receive, you create problems as outside distractions.

Have you ever been in a situation when you were just about to receive, and suddenly some kind of problem interfered so that you weren't able to? If this is true for you, take a deeper look at what fear might be creating these outside problems.

Close your eyes and go down into yourself. See the area where you think the fear is and just dwell there. Imagine what it could be. As you get in touch with yourself and allow your feelings to come to the surface, sit there until you start becoming aware of where you might feel a little bit threatened or overwhelmed, or where you feel you would have to go into sacrifice to pay back a debt. Burn through this feeling by just feeling it until it is gone. When it goes, you will be free to receive. You may find that the feeling will come in big layers, and that throughout the course of the day you will have to burn through each layer. Be dedicated today to finding the source of what is keeping you from receiving.

64 When you are afraid of how good it can be, you create problems.

You create problems because you are afraid of receiving. You are afraid you are not worthy of what would come to you, or that what you might receive would be overwhelming.

Imagine you are the creator of your life, that you are the one ultimately responsible for the way your life is going. Take a look at your problems. You are the one creating them. Why would you want to do something like that to yourself? How could you possibly have it in for yourself so much?

Take a look at all the problems around you. Imagine you have created them, because at a subconscious level, you certainly have. They are all yours. Imagine that fear, which is the major dynamic of any problem, is at the core. Just sit there dwelling on your problem until your fear begins to emerge. As it emerges, feel it, burn through it until it disappears.

65 Your relationship is your fastest path to growth.

We do not always appreciate all the things our relationship brings to us. Many times we complain about all the negative feelings we have to go through, all of the burden, heaviness, sacrifice, and all of the lessons we have had to face. Sometimes we think, "I got into this relationship to be happy, and I've been far from it ever since the honeymoon ended." This is because relationships constantly bring up every unhealed part of ourselves so that we can mature and grow and develop as a human being. Your relationship is a constant invitation to keep evolving, to keep moving to higher understanding and deeper compassion.

Take the day just to appreciate your relationship, because your relationship leads you to deal with things that you could easily avoid if you were on your own. As negative feelings come up: feel them until they are gone, communicate until they are gone, forgive until they are gone; you will find a new level of trust within yourself, a new level of commitment, a new giving of yourself, and a new ability to receive. Your relationship is always calling this forth. So today, appreciate your partner and all those who've been around you, helping you mature by revealing those pieces in yourself that, once integrated, lead to healing.

To end a conflict, change it on the inside.

Often, the easiest way to heal outside conflict is to go within. Find the two parts of our mind that are at war, and then go back through time to when the conflict began and change the past scene. If the outside conflict is still not resolved, it means a deeper conflict situation is still inside.

Close your eyes, and feel yourself relaxing. Feel all the cares and worries of the week melting down through you, out your feet, and into the floor. Now, choose a conflict that you are experiencing, and feel yourself drifting back through time and space to where this conflict began. How old were you when this occurred? Who was with you? What did you decide about yourself, and about life? What were the other decisions you made that are now part of your belief system, the filters through which you create your present reality? If you do not like that scene, then you can change it by imagining that you are a script writer, and that you wrote the past scene for a certain purpose. What was it?

Now you have grown and learned, and there may be a much better way to succeed in that purpose. Knowing what you know now, how would you make that scene different? How you decide to realise that purpose now, and how you change the scene will become a new pattern in your mind, and will allow you to change your subconscious programming; this pattern will then begin to dictate your present reality. Remember, no matter what the situation was, or how anyone else behaved, when anyone acts in an unloving way, love is their deepest need. So if you move forward with love, its transformative power will change the scene in your mind's eyes, and thus change a pattern created in the past. What do you choose now?

What is around us in the world is like a waking dream that reflects back to us what is going on in our deeper mind.

67 The longer you hang on, the more you lose.

It is really important to know when to let go of your attachments to allow for a new birth. In any relationship, the more you hang on, the more you lose your attractiveness, and thus become a burden on your partner. If you are willing to let go of all the things you think should be, the relationship can reach a new level of partnership. You may have to let go totally, because if there is any possibility for the relationship to move forward, it will only do so through your willingness to let go.

Take a look around and see what you are hanging on to. Is it a person, an old lover, someone who's died, ... is it a project? Just let it go, and take a few days to see what comes to you. Look for something outside you to show you which way to move. Remember, even if the person comes back to you, let them go at every turn so your non-attachment allows the relationship to keep unfolding and your attractiveness to keep growing.

68 When you let go, something better always comes to you, because letting go moves you forward.

If you have been holding on to something, you have been preventing yourself from receiving. When you let go, you may receive the same relationship at a new level, or something that is true for you – both of which will make you happier.

Today is a day to let go and to welcome, to sit with a certain sense of expectancy. Have the courage to sit there, empty-handed, knowing the universe abhors a vacuum and would want to fill it immediately. Just wait expectantly, knowing something good is coming your way.

69 Every power struggle is a reminder of a place where you have been hurt.

And you are having this power struggle because you are trying to defend that old hurt so you won't be hurt again. In this new situation, your partner acts out the part of you that you pushed away, or lost, or built a defence against because you believe it hurt you, or got you into trouble. The new situation is a trigger in the present to help you remember the old hurt so it can be healed. So, the only way to the next step in your life is to reintegrate that piece. The healing of this power struggle is really the healing of an old broken heart.

Today, in this power struggle, allow yourself to feel all of the negative feelings as old feelings. Feel them through until they are gone and until nothing stands between you and your partner, until you can really embrace your partner as the person who is always giving you back a piece of your heart.

70 Feeling your feelings is the most basic form of healing.

Whatever we feel that is not powerful and loving and good is really an opportunity for healing. So when we feel bad from time to time, our willingness to feel our feelings until they are gone allows them to burn away.

Just experience your negative feelings, even exaggerating them so as to move through them. You may find layer upon layer of feelings of deadness, of the temptation to die, of numbness or emptiness. Whatever it is, just feel it, and know that it is not the truth. As you re-associate with your feelings, you learn how to be a true partner. You learn how to open yourself to receive. And you learn about commitment. So, don't be afraid to feel your feelings!

71 Forgive your mother to clear up the problem in your relationship now.

Mothers are great scapegoats. We can blame them for anything we did not receive. As a matter of fact, at some level, whatever is negative in your relationship now is some form of blame on your mother for not giving you what you thought she should have. Your willingness to forgive your mother is your willingness to make your relationship here and now a lot better.

Today, write out the problem in your relationship. You might even write out a number of them out. Next to each problem write a response to the question: "What have I not forgiven my mother for?" In the final column, for each of the grievances against your mother, ask yourself these questions: "Would I hold this against myself? Would I use this to stop me now in my relationship?" If the answer is no, you are free, your mother is free, and your relationship is free.

72 Every expectation is a fear of the future.

Expectations and demands come out of a sense of inadequacy, which is, at some hidden level, always defending against the future. You rush forward into the future with your expectations, but you have little, if any, ability to receive or enjoy. Or you don't bother moving forward at all because nothing could meet the level of your expectation. Either form of behaviour – rushing into the future without being able to receive, or not even bothering to move – is a way of defending against taking the next step. No matter how much you rush forward, you still have one foot nailed to the floor, and so you go in circles. But you think, "At least I know where I'm going."

Today, imagine that you put your future into the hands of your Higher Self, and just let that be your affirmation all day long: "I put myself into the hands of my Higher Self." Know you are well taken care of, that every problem is in your Higher Mind's hands, and everything will move forward to be in your best interest.

73 Feeling rejected may be a defence against feeling guilty.

One of the purposes of rejection is it can hide guilt. The guilt may be for something we have done, or it may be from something in the past. For instance, a great deal of feeling rejected in childhood comes about as a result of a child's guilt for feeling attracted to the parent or sibling of the opposite sex. At the same time, the child also fears getting too close to them. As a result, he or she often creates some kind of rejection or separation so as to avoid dealing with the constant feeling of being bad or guilty.

Realise that any feeling of rejection is really just a defence or a cover to hide feelings of unworthiness. Then know that these feelings hide feelings of guilt.

Is this guilt coming from something in the past, the present, or both? If you were to know what you are feeling guilty about, it probably had to do with you and someone else. And, if you were to know what occurred between you and that person to create this feeling of guilt that is now holding you back, what could it have been? Take your guilt now and place it in the hands of God. Since God sees you as innocent, it would be arrogant of you to see yourself as guilty. You would then be using your guilt to hold yourself back from moving forward and taking the next step. Today is a day to forgive yourself and to allow yourself to be free from the guilt and rejection.

74 The extent to which you are independent is the extent to which you are denying your dependence.

Independence is a stage of growth that we go into after we have been dependent. Typically, we go into independence because we have been so heartbroken or jealous that it was too painful for us to remain dependent any longer, or to be put in a position where we could be rejected again; or, we burned out by being in sacrifice to other people, so we decided to become independent and not allow ourselves to be manipulated again.

The degree of your independence is also the extent to which you disassociated from your feelings, and it is the extent to which you did not finish the business of your dependence but ran away from it. An independent person has made a choice to be out of touch with these feelings so they do not have to deal with situations where they could feel hurt again.

You can tell how independent you are by how much you move away from people who are needy. The extent to which you are revolted by them, is the extent to which you are feeling repulsed by your own neediness.

If you are independent, you will tend to attract people around you who are dependent, because they will reflect this part of your mind for you. Reach out to these people, not from a place of sacrifice, but from giving. Realise as you are giving, as you are reaching out with the truth to them that you are also helping yourself by getting in touch with your old feelings, and finishing the business of your dependence.

75 The final stage of independence is the dead zone.

In our culture we have been taught that the final stage of growth is independence – but in truth, independence is just a stage along the way to interdependence or partnership. To move into interdependence we have to be willing to adopt a completely different set of guidelines regarding the rules for the game of life. What was very successful in independence will prove to hold us back in interdependence.

In the dead zone we do things because we are supposed to do them – not because we choose to. Although independents are the great rebels of life and won't allow themselves to be enslaved, they are really hiding a sacrificer inside themselves.

The final stage of independence is a stage of deadness that I affectionately call the dead zone. This stage feels like being stuck, like being in a pattern. In the dead zone, you feel like a failure, no matter how much of a success you are to other people. You are also tempted to die because you feel such exhaustion and such a deep weariness. This is because you have not been able to receive; your feminine side has not been fully healed yet, which is the side of you that receives. It is the side that will nurture you and give you the fuel to carry on.

It is here in the dead zone that the essential character of independence is hidden – it is that of competition. At this stage you become such a great competitor that you don't even bother to compete, because when you are the best, why bother competing with anyone else? But competition still drives you forward. It makes you work, but it does not allow you to receive your reward.

If you are in the independent stage, it is time to consider switching to a higher level of growth. Here you will have greater challenges and greater risks and bigger lessons. But it will get you out of the dead zone.

Today, make the choice: "I am finally willing to go to this higher stage. I don't know what it is. Please teach me." You can ask this of the Universe or of God. Your willingness will allow yourself to be taught, and you will be thrown into relationships where you can begin to learn what true interdependence is.

76 There is no pain or problem my love could not heal.

My love has the power to join, the power to support and to heal the world. My love can make a bridge over separation, over every problem to join with any person who is separated from me. My love can fill that emptiness, because behind my love is the power of the universe, and the power of miracles. I will give my love today, and the world around me will be healed.

Someone is specifically calling for your help. If you cannot see or talk to them, visualise them in front of you. Pour your love into them as you see them. Fill them with your love. See them happy and healed and whole. Even if you speak no words of love, the love of the Universe will pour through you to your friend who is in need.

77 When things get worse, it may be because they are getting better.

This is often the case when healing occurs; the situation feels more painful and looks messier, but what is going on is true healing. When birth occurs, it can be very messy, with a lot of screaming and pain, but new life is coming into the world.

If, after sincerely trying to join with your partner, you reach out to them and things seem to blow up, you may feel you have failed, and so decide not to bother trying again. But often that explosion is the very sign that you have healed the surface layer, and so what is hidden underneath will blow up to the surface. Because you have succeeded in joining your partner, that deeper pain can now come to the fore. When this occurs, reach out once again to your partner and join them, and then this layer of pain will be healed. Each time you hit another mountaintop of success, it is only a matter of time before you venture down into the next valley of conflict. There, a healing will take place which will bring you to a new mountaintop, and soon ...

It is time to take a new attitude toward pain. Take a much deeper look at everything you are experiencing today, because at the heart of it may be a new birth, a new healing for your partner and yourself.

78 The ultimate goal is total dependence on the universe.

The initial stages of growth are dependence, independence, and interdependence. But the highest stage is radical dependence on God. This is the form of consciousness where you know that good things are coming to you and that your openness to receiving allows many blessed events to come your way. Like the birds of the air and the lilies of the field, you will be supported, loved and taken care of.

The thought of such radical dependence terrorises us. We have learned to be in control and independent. And now, as we move forward, we are being asked to give up control and to learn greater lessons of trust and of letting ourselves rest in the Hands of God.

Today, every time you see yourself trying to do something, choose that it be done for you or through you rather than by you. Every time you find yourself trying to get out of a difficulty, get out of your own way and trust that it will be done for you. It is time to be, rather than do. Just trust and open yourself. Allow yourself, like a little baby, to be in the Hands of God, totally loved and cared for in every way.

79 When you feel yourself in contraction, reach out and give to someone.

We contract when we feel hurt, self-conscious, embarrassed, ashamed, mortified, guilty, or fearful. But one of the simplest ways to heal this is to reach out and give to someone to whom you feel called to give. This is a leadership principle: The other is more important than my problem of self-torture. As I reach out to them we are both healed.

When you feel hurt or are in any form of difficulty, ask yourself who is in even greater pain, and see who pops into your mind. Feel yourself reaching out to them. As you reach out to give to them, you will find yourself once again in the flow. This is an act of leadership, and of love.

80 A problem occurs in the relationship when there is a fear of taking the next step.

The very easiest way to move through any problem is not to get caught up in solving it. When a problem occurs the answer comes with it. Your willingness to trust this and move forward allows you to know what the answer is. Once you have taken the next step, what was a problem may just be something to handle, or it may disappear completely. But it will no longer be a problem for you.

Choose the three juiciest problems in your life. Take five minutes in the morning to look at the first problem, and say, "I will not be fooled by this problem. I know this is just the result of fear, and I can step through this fear by saying 'yes' to the next step in my life. I trust this next step will come to me. I know that it is better than this. I will not be caught by this problem because it is not the truth." In the afternoon, choose the second problem, and spend another five minutes on it. In the evening, do this once again. You will be very happy with the results!

81 Your expectations compensate for hidden needs.

Your expectations come out of your demands; your demands come out of your needs; and your expectations are a defence against your needs, a way of acting as if you are not dependent. Acting in a defensive and an independent mode, you demand the situation reflect your picture of how reality should be. But any type of defence, expectations included, always leads to failure and the very thing you were trying to defend against – a place of frustration or disappointment, where you begin to experience your own needs and neediness.

Your demand is a clue to the area of your need, which cover up old feelings of sadness, abandonment, and lack of bonding. Communicating about your feelings is the beginning of bonding again. Today, practice giving up your demands and communicate truly about what you need (which often satisfies the need itself). Even if communication does not succeed in fulfiling your needs, it will give you the confidence to deal with them openly without trying to control others.

82 Pain and conflict in the relationship come from broken rules that you established.

You may not have told your partner that you had these rules, but you think if they *really* loved you, they should have known. We set up these rules to protect ourselves from being wounded again. But as you know, rules are meant to be broken, just as all this pain is meant to be healed. So your partner will unintentionally (or, intentionally) break your rules just for your healing and benefit. Be willing to give them up. Give up your protection and feel the pain that you have buried. Let it come out for your healing, growth, and your ability to partner on a new level. Be willing not to blame your partner for breaking your rules, or for not loving you. Actually feel a sense of appreciation that they have triggered this pain, which you would never have dealt with if they had not broken your rules.

Write down every rule you have about relationships, about how you should be treated, about sex, about love. This could be one of the funniest days of your life when you see what your rules are and how contradictory some of them are. At the end of the day, after having shared these rules with your partner, who probably will really enjoy them, burn them. And in burning them, let them go.

Now it is time to choose principles for your relationship. Principles create dialogue and they are both resilient and flexible. They are not meant to be broken as rules are, but to be goals that are life sustaining.

83 In any conflict, both people are feeling the same thing, even though they may be acting out opposite behaviours.

For instance, one person may be a spendthrift and the other a miser. But both people are feeling the same sense of scarcity, the fear that there is not enough. The spendthrift compensates for this feeling by spending excessively. The miser pinches pennies as a protection against the feeling of scarcity. Both are trying to protect themselves against the same thing.

So if you are in touch with your feelings, you can then be in touch with the feeling underneath your partner's behaviour. Your willingness to begin communicating about this feeling allows you to find a common place, a beginning of something that you share. This is the beginning of healing – because once you find an area of common connection, you are on your way to moving forward together.

Choose a person with whom you are in conflict, and ask yourself, "What is the feeling underneath my behaviour?" Now take a look at their behaviour and see if their feeling fits with yours. If you come to a feeling of anger, realise anger is a defence that protects an even deeper feeling. Whatever your deeper feeling, be willing to begin communicating with the purpose of moving ahead.

84 When your fear of resistance is too strong for you to move toward your partner, ask for Heaven's help.

We know moving toward our partner is the answer to every problem, but there are times when we are in so much pain, or we are so exhausted, or we have so much resistance, that we feel we just cannot take one more step in any direction. That is the time to ask for Heaven's help. Ask for renewed strength to take another step toward your partner. Many times that strength will carry you right to the heart of your partner. Sometimes the resistance or the pain may be so strong you have to ask for Heaven's help every step of the way. But that means you are healing a chronic pattern within you, a layer of deep pain. Be willing to ask for help every step. Let grace carry you forward and energise you.

In any situation today where it seems too difficult for you to move toward anyone, ask for Heaven's help to move toward each of these people until you feel once again you have a sense of closeness and a sense of common purpose.

So, if you have been acting out the role of the hero in your relationship, notice how you need to find situations where you can demonstrate your greatness, and thus find a way to save the day. That means your partner has to play the role of the villain, or of someone who constantly needs to be saved – not a happy choice. Taking centre stage as the star, means always setting up a subtle competition where your partner has to play the supporting role. But if you learn to be more in touch with your feelings and yourself, no one will have to play a supporting role in your play.

Every role is a compensation for the feeling that you are no good. If you feel bad, you act badly – so various roles can emerge. You could be the villain, or your bad feelings could set up a situation which generates the role of victim, the one who needs to be saved. If you have set up a situation where you are the shining hero, ask yourself, "What is the purpose of my taking on the role of hero?" Whatever your situation, be willing to look underneath any role you are playing for the bad feelings involved. In a hero role, as in any role, you cannot receive because all the rewards go to the role. And if you cannot receive, you cannot go forward.

Your willingness to commit to your partner being the star also, is a step in commitment that moves you both forward. Be willing to give up whatever your role is, to re-associate with your feelings. You will then have the capacity to move forward with your partner, and have a greater ability to receive.

Today, begin to look under your hero costume. How big the hero role is indicates how much bad feeling lies underneath. Or take a look at the villain or the needy person in the relationship. That is the extent of how bad you and they similarly feel inside. You may have been caught up in this role since you were a child, fantasising or creating situations of need or villainy all of your life in order to fulfil yourself. Be willing to communicate about the feelings your role may be covering so both you and your partner can move forward together.

86 You cannot be a victim unless you are trying to get revenge.

One of the strongest, hidden dynamics in any victim situation is the search for revenge. But the truest way to give up being a victim is to give up your need for revenge.

As children, when we did not get what we wanted, we felt rejected and sometimes threw tantrums and hurt ourselves to get revenge. "I'll never eat again ... or I'm going to stop breathing ... or I'll run away forever and then you'll be sorry, mummy and daddy." As teenagers feeling the heartbreak of our first relationship, we thought, "I'll get into a car accident and die. Then they'll know how much I meant to them, but it will be too late." It sounds childish, but this attitude is still going on in any victim situation. In sickness, injury, or failure, we are actually getting revenge on someone.

Sit quietly and let a present victim situation such as illness, loss, heartbreak or accidents come to your mind. Then ask yourself, "Who am I getting revenge on?" Then let other victim situations come to your mind, and ask the same question. You see the irony is, you are only using someone else to hold yourself back. Be willing today to see how revenge is a form of avoiding the next step. It is a power struggle in which we hurt ourselves in an attempt to emotionally blackmail someone, to get back at them. And it will not work. Even if you win the power struggle, you may have to go so far as to die as a victim to get your point across.

87 Every step you take toward your partner is a step in personal power.

If your partner is in need and you step toward them, you do so out of your fullness. Or, if you feel that is too difficult, you can step forward by asking for Heaven's help to move toward them. Even in situations where you are in pain and your partner is doing fine, if you step toward your partner, you will feel stronger and begin to move through your pain.

Today, consciously empower yourself by stepping toward your partner continuously.

88 Everyone's actions reflect your choices.

This realisation is a major step in maturity, and in understanding the power of your mind and the nature of the subconscious. When people realise this is true, they are sometimes tempted to feel guilty for events that have taken place. Yet, everyone is innocent because everyone makes these choices mutually, somehow believing that what they are choosing will bring them happiness. Sometimes the choices we make are mistakes, but this is not a reason for guilt, which is a trap of the ego to dis-empower us. Mistakes actually provide an opportunity for connection – to correct the mistake and join others.

When we make choices, we do so one hundred percent. If one person in the situation desisted from agreeing, this would change the consensual reality, and then the situation would not occur. You could choose to see that person as a reflection of your mind and make a choice to help and empower them and you at the same time.

This means that, in your relationship, you are responsible not only for your behaviour and feelings, but also for your thoughts – the choices you are making in your mind. Your thoughts create the scenario in your relationship. The problem is that most of the time we are totally unaware of our thoughts. In any given two-mile stretch of road that you might drive, you think an average of two thousand thoughts. How many of those thoughts are you conscious of? As you become aware of your thoughts, you become more empowered, and you make better choices.

Now is the time to realise that your experience in the relationship is the result of a choice you are making, even though not all of these choices may be conscious ones. Ask yourself: "What would be the purpose of having my partner act this way? What does it allow me to do? What is it I do not have to do? Who am I getting back at by having this happen? What old debt does it pay off for me?"

Today, get in touch with what choices you are making in your relationship. Let go of any guilt that comes up, and then consciously see what you want. All day long let your affirmation be "I choose [what ever it is you want in your relationship]." To do that once with full sincerity empowers you to change both the subconscious and unconscious minds. As you choose, feelings and beliefs that stand between you and what you want may come up. Be willing to choose again in the face of whatever feeling is present. Choose what it is you want. Do not stand for less.

89 Your complaints are a direct attack on yourself.

Every time you complain, you are saying you do not have the power to make a difference in the situation. And of course that is foolish, because you have a great deal of power. When you are complaining, you are making yourself small. There is a risk you are afraid to take, and there is some action you are not taking, which you have been called to do. By your complaints, you are becoming part of the problem. You are saying "This problem is real, and I'm stuck with it, and I can't do anything about it." Au contraire!

Today is the day to see where you can make a difference. Catch yourself in every complaint you make, and instead of complaining, take a step forward, and reach out to someone, or forgive someone, or take action to make the situation better. As the poet, E. E. Cummings wrote, "I'd rather teach one bird how to sing than ten thousand stars how not to dance."

90 Any judgement you have against another is a judgement against yourself.

You cannot judge unless you are feeling guilty about something. Otherwise, you would simply see that a mistake has been made, and that with your support, the mistake can easily be corrected. But when you feel guilty about a mistake or something similar you have repressed, then your guilt will come out as a judgement against someone else. This will keep you stuck with your guilt, and what you have judged. But if you will only forgive, you will not have to search your subconscious mind to find where all your hidden guilt is. Forgiveness not only releases your partner or the person you have judged and reestablishes their innocence, it reestablishes your innocence. What you, or they, have done is not a sin. It is just a mistake.

What we get stuck in, we call sin because it seems unforgivable, almost impossible to correct. But, actually, everything can change – in our minds. A mistake can be corrected. But when we identify something as a sin, we obsess about it, coming back to it again and again in our minds, until eventually we bury our guilt and project it out onto others.

Take a look at the person you are judging the most. Just for a moment imagine that the very thing you are judging them about is true about you. Dwell on that quality until you actually begin to realise, "Yes, this is guilt I have hidden away – but this is not true about me, either. I'm not going to hold this against them, because I'm not going to hold it against me." Getting in touch with that hidden feeling and burning it away, or just refusing to hold it against them so you yourself are set free, allows the whole situation to move forward.

91 The extent to which you are indulgent is the extent to which you are in sacrifice.

When you indulge yourself in food, work, sex, alcohol, drugs and so on, you are compensating for all the sacrifice you are doing. If you were just truly giving, you would have to be truly receiving. Then there would be no need to indulge yourself – which wears you out as much as your sacrifice does. Indulgence sets up a vicious circle of indulgence/ guilt/ sacrifice. Indulgence leads to guilt, and then you appease your guilt by going into sacrifice. After you have been in sacrifice for a while and burned yourself out, you feel it is okay to indulge yourself, to do exactly what you want with a certain level of rebellion or resentment to those you feel in sacrifice to.

Look at the areas where you have indulgences or addictions. Are you a workaholic? Are you indulging in, or addicted to food? Now, take a clear look at the place where you feel you are not in the centre of your own life – because where you are not in the centre, where you are not being true to yourself, you are in sacrifice. So come to the centre of your life, and move out of the indulgence and sacrifice. Imagine there is a centre in you. What percentage from zero to a hundred did you get off your centre? (Usually readings of thirty to eighty percent reflect heavy sacrifice, while eighty to a hundred percent reflect self-destructiveness in the cycle of sacrifice and indulgence.) What experience took you off your centre? Go back there now, and choose to once again centre yourself. At this point, from your centre, you can give the gift the people around you really need. This gift is part of who you are.

92 Anger is blaming the other person for what you believe you have done.

Our anger is the attempt to project onto someone else the feelings we have about ourselves. In our anger we pretend that the very quality we are angry about has nothing to do with us, that we, of course, are innocent. But actually, it is our fear and guilt that drives our anger and our attack. All anger lacks integrity. Although, if we feel angry, there is an integrity in expressing what we are experiencing. But then, after having done so, it is important not to use our anger to try to control the situation.

Be aware that as soon as we go to second and third and fourth statements about our anger, we are trying to control the situation by blaming our partners or the people around us for things we feel badly about. When a parent gets angry at a child for acting in a certain way, or has fears about what the child will grow up to be, their fear and anger come from beliefs they hold about themselves. With more healing, there would be more flexibility and creativity in how the parent treats the child.

Be willing to recognise that what the other person is acting out for us is something we feel bad about. Recognising this can be the beginning of communication, and of a new level of honesty and integrity. Recognise that if the person is not acting out of love, they are calling for love, and if we are willing not to judge, we can offer a support that can totally transform the situation.

93 All anger comes from lack of trust and past hurts.

We imagine the present situation is like the past, and the places where we were hurt in the past will be exactly the same in the present. So we get angry. But if we were to bring trust into the situation so that when we felt the temptation to get angry, we would just acknowledge those deeper feelings inside us, and the fear and pain would begin to unfold in a healing fashion. The pain then becomes the vehicle for communication which can provide a much bigger reward in the situation than the anger can bring – because while anger might allow us to win the battle, it will cause us to lose the war. What we get angry at, we reinforce and so we get stuck with it. And even if we gain control, the other person's loss in the battle makes them unattractive to us.

Use your trust to recognise that this situation is not like the past. Even though it looks as if you might be hurt, this is the chance for facing that old feeling and chronic pattern so you can step forward with a new level of confidence that the situation will turn out for the very best.

94 Anger is always an attempt to control through guilt.

Anger, with its aggression and sometimes violence, is always an attempt to control, to move the situation our way, and to make the other person feel guilty. As such, it is always a form of blackmail. Anger says, "Look at what you have done to me ..." or, "You should have done it better ..." or, "It is your fault I am this way ..." or, "You better do it better and take care of me better." So anger is a form of control whereby we can win the battle but lose the war, because the more guilt we sow, the more resentment we reap. We may control a person through our anger or through their guilt for a long time, but finally they will explode, and we will have lost them.

If you are using your anger as a tool to hide your fear and get your way, it is time to start talking about what you are feeling instead of exploding at every opportunity. Talk about your fear so you can move to higher levels of confidence and greater levels of satisfaction. Share that first level of anger, but then immediately share the feeling underneath it, and the feeling underneath that until you feel completely at peace. Sometimes you may even get in touch with where the situation or feeling seems to begin, and sharing about that and its effect on you will bring a healing balm. Your risking will bring you forward.

95 Anger is a way of controlling to get our needs met.

When we get angry, it is because things are not going our way. Sometimes we use our anger to demand things go our way so we get to be right or have our needs met first. But anger sets up a pattern that locks us into our neediness; we fall into a vicious cycle of needs, anger, fear, and needs again. When we get angry, we think other people will get angry also, so we become afraid, and fear is one of the aspects that create needs.

When we are willing to stop using anger as a form of control and to start talking about our fear that our needs will not be met, it is more likely that they will be. Sometimes just communicating about our needs helps to fulfil them. By taking that risk in communication, we build up our own maturity. Whether we get a particular need met or not, we have moved forward and empowered ourselves.

Take a close look. You may be in the habit of anger. And it is not really working because you are alienating the very one who could meet your needs. So instead of using your anger, speak what you are feeling, and move toward your partner to join them.

Today, find the person you are angriest with. Imagine beside them the person you love the most – it may be the same person. Look at the person you love the most, look beyond their body, their personality, and their mistakes, and see the light shining inside them. Imagine your light and their light joined together. Rest in that feeling of peace for a while. Now, take a look at the person you are really angry with. Look past their body, their personality, and their mistakes, and see the essence of them, that light, that spirit shining inside them. Now, joined with the person you love, feel your lights moving to join with the other person's light. When all of the lights have joined, feel yourself resting in this place of peace.

96 Anger hides grace.

Have you ever noticed that sometimes when you get angry at your partner for the littlest things, it is when they've wanted to lavish you with love? So often, in our smugness about really telling them what is bugging us, we choose the anger and do not even recognise we missed an opportunity to feel joyful. If you keep your awareness about you, you will see you really have a choice between your anger and receiving their love.

Anger is generated from judgement. If we pay attention to our anger, we can see we have a choice in the matter. The natural physiological reaction of anger lasts about four and a half minutes. After that, it is something we harbour and choose to feel. Judgement and anger hide the opportunity for grace, for something miraculous. If we are aware and willing instead of judging, we can use the opportunity to offer support and love, to feel joyful and thereby be a channel of grace in the situation. Every time we offer grace, we have naturally received it in order to proffer it. If we make the choice for grace instead of grievance, we can become an emissary of transformation and healing – an emissary for Heaven.

Today, take the time to notice where, in your judgement, you are either withdrawing or becoming aggressive. Make the choice for love and grace. Look back in your life to significant times of withdrawal or attack and in your mind's eye, make a new choice for grace. In offering grace, the situation may finally be transformed.

97 Commitment opens you to receiving.

Your commitment is your choice to fully give yourself as much as you possibly can. Giving and receiving are naturally tied together, so the more you move into commitment – the more you give to something – the more you receive from it. The more you give to your partner, the more you recognise your partner's beauty and their gifts and how great they are. Giving to them is what allows you to have the eyes of love that can truly see how wonderful they are. So your commitment, your giving, your love determines how great they are.

How significant a situation is for you depends on how much you have given yourself to it. Any situation where you have gone beyond yourself and exceeded what you have known yourself to be, moves you into an altered state of consciousness. By giving that much, you are open to receiving great gifts of joy and ecstasy. If you are not receiving in a relationship, look at the level of your commitment.

Today, look at a situation in which you wish you were receiving more. Look at how you can give yourself more fully. Sacrifice does not count. Remember, sacrifice is counterfeit commitment. Making the choice to give of yourself allows you to enjoy the situation more. The more you give, the more you enjoy yourself, and the more you receive. Commitment is a choice for giving.

Commitment means being true to yourself.

When we commit, we give of ourselves so much that we begin to know our true essence and what really matters to us. This knowledge comes, not from holding back and complaining, but from giving above and beyond what the contract says, beyond what is expected of us. Through commitment you get to know the richness and depth of yourself. You get to know the self to whom things come easily, and yourself as your best self.

Remember a time when you felt you had given yourself one hundred percent, with no expectations, a time when you had gone beyond yourself. Go back to that situation. Feel the feelings there. Hear what people were saying to you. What did things look like there? Just revel in that a moment. Now bring that feeling up into your present situation. What is it you would like to do differently now? How much more would you choose to give yourself in this situation? The feeling of joy that comes through giving yourself totally can be yours. Total giving begins to unlock grace and hidden resources. It is the stuff miracles are made of.

99 No problem can withstand commitment, which means giving yourself one hundred percent.

Any problem points to a conflict in our mind in which parts of us are vying for different needs to be met. But no problem can withstand the choice and commitment to join all the parts together. When a problem begins to unfold, and you take the first step giving one hundred percent of yourself, one step will lead to another. A certain flow will emerge because when you give yourself one hundred percent, things come to you easily. Doors open. Opportunities occur. Luck happens. No problem can withstand the power of your choice to give yourself one hundred percent.

Look at the major problem confronting you and ask yourself how much you are giving yourself in that situation. When did you withdraw the other percentage of yourself? Was it long ago in the past or just a short time ago? Today you can make the choice to give yourself one hundred percent in this situation. Nothing can withstand your giving yourself that much. You have the power to totally transform your experience by your commitment. Total commitment creates a state of vision in your life.

100 Your pain may be a defence against your sexual energy.

We may be embarrassed about our sexual energy because we feel guilty about how we have used it in the past, or about being so sexual. We feel as if we could not handle the attention, or we would not know how to say no ... and it certainly would be a clutter if everyone of the opposite sex, including dogs, cats, and horses, followed us home. But to feel your own energy is to experience something rich and healing, something that will then "youthen" you and be a gift to your partner. As you move forward in consciousness, your sexual energy grows; and as it grows, it empowers you to move into these higher areas of consciousness. Your sexual energy is a good part of your fuel for growth and evolution.

You can move through your pain easily today by your willingness to feel your sexual energy, and you can make it safe by the amount of love you give with it. All joy contains this kind of electrical, exciting energy.

101 Heartbreak is an act of revenge.

To experience heartbreak means we have been on the losing end of a power struggle. So we use our heartbreak as a form of emotional blackmail to get back at the other person. We get revenge on them by bleeding on their doorstep, saying, "This person can't be so good if this is what they have done to me. I will stand on their doorstep for ever and ever as a monument to what a rotten person they are."

Today, acknowledge your heartbreak as another step in the power struggle. Revenge is a place of hardened power struggle. Our heartbreaks are just an example of this kind of calcification. Forgive the people who seem to have broken your heart – including yourself. Do not use another to hold yourself back.

102 What is missing in your relationship is what you are unwilling to put into it.

What would you like more of in your relationship? Romance? Love? Abundance? Then what are you waiting for? Maybe you have been expecting your partner to bring a certain thing into the relationship. But if you see the relationship needs something, and you want it there, obviously you are the one called to give it. So stop complaining and start giving.

In a relationship, different people bring different gifts. Bring what it is you want in the relationship in the most creative way possible. Your creativity will be your joy, you will have fun, you will open yourself, you will know yourself as giving and receiving, you will grow in your own confidence, and the relationship will move forward by what you have given it.

And remember, it is not about simply giving the form of what you want, like sex for example. It's about giving more of your sexual energy to make sex more attractive. Sometimes when your partner does not want sex, it signals a place where you may have withdrawn from them sexually. Move into a higher level of sexual energy and inspire your partner.

What does your relationship seem to need the most? Over the next week, give something related to that need in a different and creative way every day.

103 What you think you need is what you are called to give to the other.

This is the easiest way to heal. Usually, our biggest complaint against our parents is that we had needs they did not meet. But what we needed from our parents is actually the very thing we came to give them. And when we give this, we resolve our belief that they came here to meet our needs. One of the most important aspects of our conspiracy against ourselves not to grow is waiting for someone else to fill our needs, when our needs are the very things that show us what we are to give.

Take a look at what you feel you need, and take the responsibility yourself for bringing it into the relationship. If there is something you need at work or in your family, you be the one to bring it there. Being the leader in this will make you very happy by being in a position where you can really do some good for yourself and others.

104 **Considering how hard it seems to be to change within yourself, it is foolish to expect to change someone else.**

And even when we do succeed, we lose, because the person loses their attractiveness for us. The easiest way to get someone to change is to change yourself, to move forward yourself – it is an irresistible call to your partner to join you. Where someone in our world is stuck, it merely reflects a part of our subconscious mind that is stuck and afraid to change.

Who is the main person in your life whom you want to be different? This very person represents an area in you that has been hardened and unwilling to change. Today, ask for Heaven's help in stepping forward to give this very thing. You take the step forward and be willing to give what you wanted of someone else. Your happiness is at stake and it is in your hands.

105 Busyness is a major device for trapping ourselves in the valueless, which is used to avoid, to hide our joy and our gift of ease.

Even though technology has been produced to save us time, somehow the projects we undertake (the busyness, the activities and hobbies we engage in, and the events that we go to) all seem to proliferate. The more technology we gain, the busier we seem to become. Often this busyness takes over our relationships. We move from one activity to another and do not take the time just to enjoy our partner. In the midst of all this, take time to realise what has value for you, what will last you for all eternity versus what is just a flash in the pan.

Busyness is used to compensate for our valuelessness. All the activities are used to prove that we have worth. All of this activity is just a form of denial that will fail at some point allowing all the feelings of valuelessness to surface along with its encumbent feelings of failure and death temptation.

Look today at what busyness you have been using to distract yourself from spending time with your partner. You may be doing things together, but you may not be coming together. Be willing to realise that your busyness and your valuelessness may be distracting you from building up your heart and meaning in your life. Think of yourself twenty years from now. What will this activity have meant then? Think of your last day of life. Would this activity be so important compared with spending time with your beloved? Be willing to let go of the extraneous busyness and stop using valuelessness as an excuse to avoid being happy with your partner.

106 Under every role is a temptation to die.

A role is a hard outer shell that can cover a lot. It is a piece of our character we began to take on in a situation where we felt like we wanted to die. We felt we were valueless, a total failure, so we gave up our selfhood and took on a role. But no matter how much we have succeeded in this role, we are never nurtured by the reward because a role does not let you receive.

A role and its rules may help a child early in life to have a good sense of character and even to learn right from wrong. But later on in life those rules become the armour that weighs us down, the heaviness that exhausts us because we cannot receive. We are doing it because we think we are supposed to, not because we choose it; we are doing the right thing for the wrong reason. Everyone around us may think we are a great success, but we feel worn out, we feel like a mere shell, a failure, unworthy or even a fraud – the very feelings we were trying to compensate for and defend against when we took on the role. The role looks good, but it will weigh you down and kill you.

If you are getting to a place of death temptation – which is at the bottom of every role we have – do not be frightened of it. Running away from the feeling of wanting to die simply empowers it. Face it squarely, but feel the feelings until they are gone, knowing it is the way through and that at the other end, there is a place of breakthrough. As you move past the death temptation, what was a role for you now becomes real. Now you can regain the centre you lost so long ago.

Or instead of feeling the temptation until it is gone, a quicker way is with all your will to choose life. In your imagination march right up to the death temptation and walk through it. As you do so the temptation will fall away and you will be free. The first time you do this is really the only time the death temptation can frighten you. If you need to, get a friend to help. Imagine the death temptation is halfway across the room and walk with your friend supporting you up to it and through it. The relief is just what you needed.

107 How another is giving to you is how they would like to be given to.

Have you ever noticed that people often give you the gifts they would love to have? Take a look at what the people closest to you give you when they give you gifts, at how they support you. This is how they would love to be given to.

If you observe your partner closely, you will be able to give to them in a way that allows them to feel truly loved. For instance, if your partner is always telling you "I love you," you know to say that back to them. Does your partner support you by doing things for you? Then give to them in the same way. Does your partner touch you a lot? Well, that is what they would really love.

Study your partner. When they truly give to you, they give you what they would love to have. This is a key to helping people really feel they are loved.

108 All relationship triangles arise from the belief that we cannot have it all in one relationship.

We all have limiting beliefs that we cannot have it all in one relationship. We have been told to grow up, that we cannot live in a fairy-tale world where we are totally happy and have everything we want.

The belief that we cannot have it all comes from a deeper belief that we cannot have our mother and father's love equally. This belief points to the imbalance of the families we were born into and the lack of bonding we all had to face as children, which our parents also had to face. Typically, we were fused with one parent and polarised from the other. We did not know the boundaries between the parent we were fused with and ourselves; at the same time we were very distant or independent from the other. Though sometimes we will be fused with both parents and alienated from our spouse.

This imbalance leads us to believe we cannot have all good things in one relationship. For example, your career may be much stronger than your relationship, or you may succeed in your relationship but not in your career. The willingness to give everything to your relationship would allow it to give everything to you. We can re-balance those original relationships and come to know we can have our mother's and father's love equally.

Right now the lesson is for you to know you can have it all in one relationship. And in knowing that you can help others to know. Now sit quietly, relax, close your eyes, and imagine you are a child again. Imagine that between your parents and you, there is a perfect balance, a perfect triangle of light with each of you on the point of the triangle. Imagine you are receiving all of their gifts and all of their love equally, and you are giving all of your gifts and your love to them equally. Now add your brothers and sisters to the configuration in a balanced and loving way, so you get to receive all their gifts and all their love equally. In your present relationship, imagine the same thing is occurring between your partner and you and any children you might have. Imagine a perfectly balanced shape, a balance among all of you.

109 When you are in fusion, you are in sacrifice:

You do not know the natural boundaries between that person and yourself. You have no sense of where your centre is, so when these people come into your orbit, you are pulled into their orbit and out of your natural movement toward your purpose and living your own life. Typically, the person you are fused with is someone you feel you have loved all your life – your parents, mates, children. You feel you want to give them everything, you want to take care of them completely, or you want to make it all better for them.

We help and help and help, but it does not make a difference; nobody moves forward because we are in sacrifice. We have become the untrue helper. In a vicious cycle of co-dependence, you may feel you have to go thousands of miles just to have some breathing space. If you are fused with a parent, you may feel as if you have to get away from them no matter how much you love them. But only by living your own life can you truly help those around you.

Sit quietly and close your eyes. Imagine you hold in your hand the sword of truth, which cuts away only what is illusory and untrue. See the sword cutting the cords of fusion and sacrifice, leaving only what is true behind. As the untrue is cut away, imagine the lines of true love and bonding growing in its place.

You may be the type of person who only needs to cut the cord once. Or you may need to cut the cord every couple of days. You may want to cut the cord with a number of people you feel fused to, where you have lost a natural sense of boundary. As you cut the cord tying you to these people, or these activities, or possibly, these addictions, you will find you have a greater sense of freedom, and when you end the fusion, you can be more intimate.

110 Fusion happens when bonding has been broken.

We all have a need for closeness, intimacy, inclusion, and bonding. When our sense of bonding has been shattered, or when it seems to be nonexistent, we have to have some type of closeness to survive, so we choose fusion. That way we can have at least some sense of being close to people. But this is not true bonding. In fusion, we give up our own centres and our own selves. In bonding, by remaining in our centre, we naturally give the gifts of who we are and receive the gifts of who others are. Our willingness to reestablish bonding through forgiveness and through recognising the love that is there allows us to have our proper boundaries, to say no when it is true to say no, and to live our own lives.

Sit down in a relaxed position, and imagine that the cords of true connection, the cords of light and love, are connecting you with all those people with whom you feel fused. As you see those cords of connection, the cords of fusion and sacrifice naturally fall away, because they are not the truth.

111 Fusion blocks communication, because emotions are blown all out of proportion.

You feel so close to the person that there are certain things you cannot say to them. When you begin to communicate, there is a natural resistance, almost a repelling, because you feel if they were hurt by anything you said, you would feel devastated. You hurt when they hurt. You suffer when they suffer. When they are angry, it is explosive for you. When they are angry at you, it is even more explosive. This over-closeness tends to block verbal communication. You have a sense of non-verbally communicating everything back and forth. A look can speak of how much you love them or of how much they dislike what you are doing. You do not feel permission to dialogue and create healing through communication. There is only 'the glance' that says it all.

Think of the people in your life you would really have a hard time saying certain things to. These are the people you are fused with and with whom you are really unwilling to take a certain risk. Imagine that you use the sword of truth to cut the cord with them so now you can really establish a dialogue with them. If there are things you have wanted to say to these people, today is the day to say them. Whether you are fused with your lover, your mate, your parent or your child, this is the day to cut the cord of fusion and take the risk of beginning a dialogue with them.

112 Fusion blocks love.

True love really wants the very best for the other person. In love you extend yourself in a connective way, in an interdependent way. But in fusion, there is co-dependency with the other person in which neither of you moves forward. If you are the one who seems to be the helper, you are afraid for the other to get better because what would be uncovered is your dependency, the place where you are afraid to move forward. So you give to them in a way that keeps them under a certain bondage to you. If you feel in bondage to anyone then you are acting in fusion and cannot truly give help to them. You could not confront them or be tough with them for their own sake even though that is what might be needed. Fusion blocks the intimacy that generates this kind of strong communication, and your ability to say or do what is necessary to really help that person. It is a kind of counterfeit closeness that blocks your interdependency. It will not generate the growth and the healing and the nurturing that love generates. In a state of fusion, at some level, both people feel as if they are starving.

Examine your relationships. Where have you been unable to really feel free because you have not had your own centre? Have you given yourself freely or out of duty? Use the sword of truth to free yourself and communicate what needs to be said. As you communicate, give the gifts and the love you have to give, that you want to give.

113 To be fused with someone is to be withdrawn from life.

When we are fused with someone, we have left our centre to move toward a goal that is not true for us. We have made the other person the goal of our life, and thus more important than our own selves in an untrue sense. Taken off our centre, we are pulled back from life, which holds us back from truly giving and receiving. We may seem to be very generous, but actually we are in sacrifice. Or we may be giving to all kinds of people where really we need to be giving to ourselves so we could accomplish a much greater work.

In fusion, you are an untrue helper. You have withdrawn – but your willingness and commitment would lead you to your purpose and to that which would fulfil you in life.

Take a good look at the areas of your life where you are not receiving because this is where you are not truly giving yourself. In these areas, you may be in fusion, you may be living someone else's life. Come back to your own centre, and really live your own life so you do not end up in the obituaries under someone else's name.

What you see in another is what you think you are.

We bury the things we do not like about ourselves and then project them out on the world around us. If you see something positive in another, but you do not believe it about yourself, you know you have repressed that gift out of guilt or fear of being overwhelmed by it. Maybe you did not want to incur another's envy, or you were afraid to continue leading in this area of giftedness, so you pushed the gift away, but it is still lying within you in potential. Otherwise, you would not resonate with this gift in another person. In the same way, the negative things you see in people are actually what you believe about yourself. You know this because as you forgive those things within yourself, they no longer seem to bother you in others. If what you see in another is what you think about yourself, you must change your judgement on the other person. Otherwise, you will be stuck with what you see in them; and if you are stuck with that, you are in sacrifice. Be willing to forgive them and to change the judgements in yourself so a positive gift might come to the surface again.

Express appreciation to one person who inspires you with their gift. Thank them for having held the vision of this gift so you could know the gift was possible, not only in your world, but in you also. Then express appreciation to someone whom you have judged. Remember the greater the risk, the greater the breakthrough you can have. Appreciation moves you through judgement and gets the relationship unfolding again.

115 Every time you see someone as innocent, you free yourself:

Where you see others as innocent, your hidden guilt is released. Guilt keeps us feeling unworthy, it keeps us in sacrifice, it keeps us punishing ourselves. When you see someone else as guilty, you are punishing yourself. Your willingness to overlook mistakes and to see your partner as innocent will free you. Realise your partner has been doing the very best they can, given their inner and outer circumstances and their life story. Support and coaching help a great deal more than complaints.

Observe where you have been considering other people as wrong, bad, or guilty. Ask yourself, "How have I been punishing myself if I am seeing them in this way?" Take a moment and see what pops into your mind. If this kind of self-retribution is not what you want, then be willing to consider the fact that they are innocent. As a healing statement, say, "I will release myself today by your innocence. I will release myself today by my innocence." Use this as a healing statement. Then say, "I see [the person's name] as innocent. I see myself as innocent, so we may be free to walk as allies."

116 Anger is always a cover for another feeling.

The deeper feeling may be sadness, loss, hurt, rejection or vengeance. It may be a feeling of guilt, sacrifice, frustration or disappointment. It may be part of a power struggle. It may be you feel so dead you think a little anger would at least get things moving a bit. Rage is also a cover for other feelings, such as helplessness or humiliation or mortification. We summon rage to protect us from major heartbreak, jealousy, loneliness, and burn-out.

Sometimes a quick way to move through your anger is simply to ask yourself, "What is the feeling underneath this?" If you are willing to feel the feeling underneath the anger, the anger itself will immediately disappear, and you will move on to the deeper feeling that is using the anger as a defence.

Look at the person you may feel angry at, or enraged by, or irritated with, and know that every form of anger, rage, or irritation is just something that is holding you back from your willingness to change. The feelings underneath anger can lead to joining, while sharing just your anger leads to control or power struggle. Be willing to recognise and share what you are feeling underneath the anger without expecting any particular type of response from them. Your communication is for your own healing. Begin the healing dialogue today.

117 Forgiveness is giving forth.

Guilt keeps us in withdrawal. Every place where we feel unworthy, or have been in sacrifice, or where we have not valued ourselves, and every place where we have suffered loss and have not let it go is a place where we are withdrawn. In our present life, all of these losses and feelings of unworthiness show up as judgements on other people. When we forgive those around us, we are giving forth. Areas within us that have been withdrawn for years can now be given forth. As we sow, so shall we reap. Once we forgive, we move forward into the flow of life again, and we finally get to receive. As we forgive and give forth, we can feel happy. Forgiveness allows us to have all of the hidden parts come back to life.

Think of three things you are judging your partner for. Imagine the areas of judgement against your partner are actually places where you are not giving forth to them or supporting them. Truly wish to give to them in these areas. Truly wish to support your own life in these areas. As you give forth to them, you will find a natural forgiveness, and you will experience a natural flow as well as an ability to receive in these areas.

118 The point of conflict is the place of opportunity.

Your attitude is all-important because it is the direction in which you move. If you see any conflict as possibly the end of your relationship, then that is what it may be for you. But if you look at conflict as an opportunity for healing, then you could reach a new level of intimacy and integration. Look at the conflict as a gift rather than just another place of hell on earth. Realise you are going to a new level of closeness now, and that your success in the relationship has brought you to a place where you can deal with this conflict.

We actually have within each of our individual minds all of the conflicts in the world, but we are only able to deal with so many at a given time. As couples, it is only when we have reached a certain stage in strength that we can deal with certain areas of conflict. If we were to truly heal each conflict within us, the conflicts in the world around us would also heal. We would have the answer for our friends and relatives, and even for our acquaintances.

As we progress and grow in maturity, we move out from the personal conflicts in our relationship and from the conflicts of our friends and relatives to face deeper and deeper levels of conflict. Thus we can take on more and more in terms of our responsiveness. Your present level of responsiveness says that at this point, you could face this new level of conflict. Realise this is a major opportunity for your learning and your growth and that this conflict has been within, just waiting for the right time to surface.

Look at a current area of conflict as if it is a gift to you. As you change your attitude toward it, the conflict will begin to show you the natural way through it.

119 To resolve a conflict, go to a common higher purpose.

Any conflict will degenerate into a power struggle without a common higher goal. Even if you succeed in controlling your partner into doing things your way, somehow your needs would not be met and you would begin to lose interest in the other person. But if you realise that both viewpoints hold a necessary piece of the puzzle, you can create something greater together – a higher level of purpose and resolution to the conflict. So begin to examine both sides of the conflict. What common, higher goal would naturally subsume these two parts of the puzzle, integrating the aspects that seem to be at odds now?

Without necessarily dwelling on either side of the conflict, just rest quietly, letting go of all of the cares and worries of the day, and ask for the higher purpose of this conflict to come to you. The answer may pop into your mind within the first few seconds. Receiving this higher purpose is the automatic beginning of the end of this conflict. What can you lose if you gain your adversary as your ally?

120 Most negative emotion has nothing to do with the present.

We usually save up all of the feeling we did not have the courage to finish feeling, and then create experiences in our present life that give us the opportunity to release the past emotion. If we were to look a little deeper in any situation being triggered in our life right now, we would realise that most of the pain we are experiencing has nothing to do with the present situation. The present pain is just a small percent of the feelings we have been carrying around with us for a long time; they trigger off the feelings we need to get out in order to be open to life, to be able to receive from life. If these feelings are kept suppressed, they fester inside us and become poisonous, affecting our health and our willingness to enjoy ourselves and our relationships.

Look a little deeper today at any of the conflicts you are having. Realise these conflicts are being put together by old situations that carried emotions you never finished with. Whether or not you get in touch with those old situations, feel the feelings until they are completely gone. Be willing to recognise your partner and the people around you are not to blame, but they are just helping you to create this healing for yourself. They are helping you to be more open to life so you can receive and enjoy your happiness.

121 Partnership leads to creativity.

When you have moved past the power struggle stage, out of the dead zone, you enter an area where both you and your partner become more and more gifted, where you constantly receive new and greater vision. This is the stage of relationships called co-creativity. Of course, this sense of creativity, whose major dynamic is love, is an area of fulfilment and great satisfaction which brings happiness. So when we partner with someone, and bond with them, we create a kind of juice or electricity in the relationship that unfolds new gifts and talents and opportunities.

Today, think of ways to connect with your partner. Spend the day dwelling on a campaign of love. Feel your connection and love for them. In spite of any debris that might have got in the way, the love and connection are still there. This is what is important in your relationship and in life. The more you connect, the more your relationship opens itself for abundance, for happiness, for love, and for all of the good things in life.

122 Pulling away from a feeling is what makes it hurt.

If we are trying to escape pain by resisting a feeling, pulling away makes us have to work twice as hard and bury twice as much. For example, sometimes we may be unwilling to feel the loss of a loved one. So we avoid the mourning and anger that we would naturally go through in order to finish feeling the loss. And as we pull away, we actually add another feeling to the loss – the feeling of hurt or rejection. The same thing happens when we don't want to feel our guilt. The more we add other feelings to those we initially bury, the more we have to dissociate. But if we chose to feel the feeling instead of burying it inside, if we experienced it totally, it would soon be gone. We could have a new beginning and leave behind disappointments that gradually make us old and wear us down.

Today, take the opportunity to feel any feeling that comes up, negative or positive. Fully experience it. If it is a negative feeling, it will eventually burn away into a positive feeling. And to fully experience a positive feeling makes it even more positive.

123 Any problem in your relationship is a signal that a gift, talent, or opportunity wants to emerge.

A problem is a form of distraction that shows you there is a fear. But what are you afraid of? A new gift, a new talent, a new opportunity is coming to you. Would you have the courage to accept it? Is this not what you always wanted? Your willingness to choose the gift, talent, or opportunity is what lets it come forward, and makes the problem (which is just a distraction) disappear. Would it not be easier to look at your problems in this new light? Look past the problem and see what positive aspect is hiding there. Have the willingness and desire to have the gift.

Imagine this new gift, talent, or opportunity pouring down from the Heavens. Imagine the energy of it entering you, and emerging from deep within yourself. If you let yourself know what it is, you will feel it become embodied in you. But even if you do not feel this, the problem will begin to fall away, for its only purpose was to distract and delay you.

124 The person you like the least is showing you what is holding you back.

This person is called a shadow figure; they embody the shadow side of yourself – what you have hidden away and repressed in yourself. Look beyond your repulsion. These people will tend to come at you in your life to let you know about the invisible block and self-judgement that has been holding back your progress. Have you ever worked very hard, but made very little progress? This situation is the result of a belief you have about yourself, a quality you hate about yourself that you have buried inside, and which you have projected onto someone else. Your projection completely blocks you, setting up an invisible shield to your progress. So when you are confronted with a shadow figure, or when you have projected a certain quality onto your partner you cannot stand, know this quality drags behind you like an invisible anchor, holding you back. It is your self-judgement and self-hatred.

Your willingness to have your Higher Power handle the needed forgiveness with this person would release the invisible block in your life and would allow you to move forward at this very moment. Ask for self-forgiveness and a feeling of innocence and resolution for both.

125 The heart of communication is recognising that present pain is rooted in a past relationship.

We recognise this when we begin to share about what is not working or what is painful in a relationship. If you and your partner are willing to support each other, you will find neither one of you is the bad guy. The pain is not something you have caused, but it is something you could help your partner resolve. Be willing to share the misunderstandings and the past pain. Share the beliefs that have come out of your past relationships, the rules you have made because you thought you needed them to survive.

Imagine a situation in which you felt your partner caused you pain. Recognise where that pain is really coming from ... because it had to have some antecedent to be this big. Then be willing to share this recognition with your partner. As you share these things with the willingness to let them go, you will find your partner much more willing to communicate and support you.

126 The refusal of what is untrue in a relationship allows the truth to emerge.

Here is something you can constantly use in your relationship: If there is something untrue, something that is not love, happiness or abundance, you do not have to stand for it. You can use the power of your mind along with truth, and if something is not truth, you can refuse it.

Today, choose at least two areas of your relationship that are not the truth because they are not happy or joyful. For this exercise, you can also chose aspects of your relationship that are neutral or just "blah". Use the power of your mind to say, "This is not the truth. I will not accept this. What I choose is the truth. What I choose is [say whatever it is]." To say this once sincerely, sometimes has the power to remove the entire conflict, or, at least, to take one layer of the conflict away from you. Use this time and time again so you can recognise this as a principle: If it is not the truth, do not adjust to it. Do not compromise. If it is not the truth, do not choose it. Keep asking for the answer or resolution.

127 To analyse a problem is to resist the solution.

Because to analyse is to break the whole up into the little pieces, thinking you will find the answer in all the little pieces. Your thinking always happens after the fact. Really, the answer to every problem comes at the moment the problem presents itself. So we actually do not have to waste any time finding the solution; we just have to have the courage to accept it. The solution comes through your intuition, through inspiration. Most of the great inventions have been discovered in a state of reverie, where the answers just popped into the inventor's mind.

Allow yourself to sit quietly. If the answer to your problem has not just jumped into your mind in the first ten minutes, allow yourself to sit there and observe every thought that comes up – things you have to do, sexual fantasies, anything. To each of these thoughts, say "This thought reflects a goal that's keeping me from my answer." After you say that, the thought will fall away. Then, at the end of ten or fifteen minutes, ask, "Now let the answer be given to me." Your willingness to receive the answer will clear the clutter of all your thoughts. Your willingness to receive the answer is the only thing between you and the solution.

It is the power of your mind used for you. Having trust means that whatever problem you have begins to heal, because any problem is a sign of lack of trust. So bring your trust into your problem. Use the power of your mind because it naturally seeks solutions. See, feel, and hear the problem working out so that you no longer obsess about it. Trust is your answer. Trust heals all.

Take some time today to use trust for any problem that seems to be holding you back, especially in your relationship. Remember, moving your relationship forward moves every other area of your life forward. The power of your mind has to go somewhere. It can go toward the problem, or the solution. You decide.

When you opt for independence, you throw out passion.

There are two types of passion. One type comes from urgency, the other from giving yourself totally. When you opt for independence, you are opting to move away from your needs, and away from the sense of urgency. But you still have not come to the point of giving yourself a hundred percent. Dissociating from your needs and your pain means you have unfinished business with the things you are unwilling to look at inside yourself. These places of unexamined pain hold you back from giving yourself one hundred percent.

Today is a day to find your passion again. Recognise your needs, give up your defensive independence, and give yourself one hundred percent to your partner, your life, and your work. Give yourself through whatever holds you back. When you give yourself a hundred percent through the painful feelings, you will emerge with a new sense of love, of power, and of passion.

130 Giving up a judgement keeps you from being stuck with what you have judged.

Your willingness to be wrong allows things to keep moving forward. Conversely, while your judgement gives you a sense of being right, it does not move you forward. Your judgement says, "Nothing can be taught to me. I have all the answers, and I am stuck." But your willingness to give up your judgement and not to know all of the answers means you could be taught something; it allows you to see things with a greater perspective and to be shown the way in this situation. One powerful form of affirmation might be: "I hope I'm wrong, because if I'm right, this is what I get."

Take a moment to see what you are judging, to see what you are stuck with, and be willing to let it go. Imagine you placed your judgement on a little boat that went down a swiftly flowing river, moving out to sea and out of your mind. There, coming toward you, is the answer: the next step in the situation. Only when you let go of the little boat carrying your judgement will your ship come in.

131 If the past is unfinished, ghosts of old relationships will come to haunt you now.

Every lesson you have not learned with your parents, siblings, or other significant relationships will interfere with your present relationship. Those lessons can be learned now by healing your present relationship, which then will enable you to see your past relationships in another light, thus healing them. Or, sometimes it may be easier to make contact with significant people from your past to come to an understanding of the old situation in the light of your present maturity, to let go of the problem, and move forward. When the old ghosts are dispersed, the blessings and good times of the past will empower you.

Today is a day for finishing old business. Contact anyone with whom you have outstanding feuds or misunderstandings, and be willing to reach out and take the next step, apologising where necessary in order to move forward. Even if the person has died, imagine them present, and speak to them, or write them a letter.

132 Every rule covers a guilt:

If you did not have the guilt, you would not need to make a rule out of it. You would be willing to be flexible and responsive. You made a rule because, at some point, you believe you made a big mistake, and you never want to make that mistake again. But often the rule becomes the problem and stands in the way of responsiveness, and of considering what is needed in the present circumstances. So your guilt keeps you acting in the same old ritualised manner, keeping the rule no matter what the circumstance.

Take a look at the areas where you may be rigid in your relationship, where you feel, "It has to be this way for me." Realise that hidden under each of your rules is a sense of guilt. Be willing to let go of the rule and the guilt. Be willing to put a principle in its place. This will allow dialogue and responsiveness.

133 A rule is self-punishment for a mistaken belief you have about yourself.

Your rules are your disciplines, but, unfortunately, these disciplines are a form of self-punishment. They are self-punishments in that rules prevent receiving. Where you have a rule, you will not have true contact with your partner, because there is something that you feel really badly about. And your rule covers it.

Write down every rule you have in your relationship. In the column next to it, write what you have decided about yourself in relation to the rule. You can be sure that if anything in this second column is negative, you are punishing yourself in some way. So in the third column, write how you are punishing yourself. When you take a good look at what the rule is, what the mistake is, and how you are punishing yourself, you might want to make a new decision about the rules you have in your life. Awareness and making new choices are keys to healing.

134 The love in your present relationship is the process by which old pains can be healed.

It allows you to let go of old ideas about yourself and old pain. In the process of growing together, everything between your partner and you will surface so it can be healed. All of us have nice self-concepts, but sometimes they hide those which are very dark and painful. While underneath these are powerful and innocent self-concepts of true goodness, that are not merely compensations for the darkness we feel in ourselves.

This is a day of recognition for how far you have come in uncovering all those "nice" self-images that never let you receive anything. Today, examine the darker ones so the healing work can continue. Examine areas of scarcity that you may have in your life, and other areas which are painful or problematic. Imagine these as areas of self-punishment for what you believe about yourself, what you believe you deserve. Feel your gratefulness for the relationship that has brought these darker self-images to the surface for healing. Now imagine all of these dark beliefs about yourself were really there to hide your true goodness: your innocence, mastery and power. As you become aware of these deeper areas of true goodness the dark defence against them will fall away.

135 **If you have a problem, you are holding on to old pain that is rooted in old problems.**

So even if you cut away the current problem, the old root would just grow other problems. Given this, sometimes it is really helpful to realise where the root comes from, and how it manifests itself in different areas of your life as seemingly new problems.

Write down three present problems in your relationship, and beside them, identify whom from the past this problem stems. Next to that, write what the problem was with that person. Trust what pops into your mind for each category. Your intuition will give you answers your thinking and memory could never give you because they are in collusion with the ego and would never give something the ego does not want to deal with. But your intuition will constantly bring you answers that can be inspired.

Now look at what you have written. If these problems you've identified come from unfinished business, would you like to finish the business now? This could be as easy as forgiving the people in the situation, or blessing them; or, you could just let the whole thing go as not being true any more, and not worth holding you back at the present time in your life.

136 Appreciation eliminates power struggles.

The problem with power struggle is it polarises each person into opposite camps against each other. The bottom-line dynamic of power struggle, its whole purpose, is that you not move forward. So if you use something that naturally moves you forward in flow, like appreciation, the power struggle will be eliminated. If you are in a conflict with your partner, begin to appreciate them.

What are all the things you really love about your partner? Spend some time in the morning and evening thinking about those things. What are the things your partner gives you? How does your partner bless your life? Sometime during the day, communicate these things to your partner. Even if you are not in a power struggle, use this time to appreciate your partner, to tell them the things you love about them and the ways they have helped you.

Even if there is only one thing you can find to appreciate about your partner, appreciating that one thing will move you forward, and it will bless you and open you.

137 Be willing to let go of the need to consume the other to make up for the past.

Where we have past needs that weren't met by our parents or life situation, we have a tendency to want to consume our partner, to swallow them alive, to take every little thing they can give us, to overwhelm them, to overshadow them, to fuse with them, and to smother them, so we can get these needs met. All of this pushes your partner away, rather than encouraging them to move toward you. If you let go of your past needs, you will find a natural balance and openness in your relationship. Be willing today to let go of any way you may be trying to consume your partner or anyone in your life as the answer to all of your prayers.

Today, give to the person whom you are most trying to consume. Do not give to take, but out of a decision that your needy self-concepts are not the truth. You are not a child any more. You can let go of these needy personalities, these self-defeating self-concepts. Value the truth and yourself today.

138 There is no such thing as a broken heart; it is really a form of tantrum.

We feel broken-hearted because our loved ones have not acted in the way we wished them to. So we take our hearts out and threaten to break them into a thousand pieces, thinking, "They'll be sorry now." But no one can make you feel anything you do not choose to feel, or that you are not already feeling at some level. If you were willing to let the situation be different from what you think it should be, then you could use the great amount of emotion that comes up to give through it. You could enter a new birth in your life, and step into a whole new level of love, and sense of confidence and empowerment.

Today is a day to regain yourself, to go back to your heartbreak situations, and use that opportunity. Instead of pulling back from the person, or going into another layer of power struggle, imagine giving through all your pain, whether your partner does what you wish or not. At that level, you would find yourself reconnecting wires in your heart, in your mind, and sometimes in your genitals, that have long since been cut. You will find yourself feeling a new surge of vitality, a renewal, a new birth, a new chapter in your life.

139 The more unlovable the behaviour, the greater the call for love.

Your willingness to support people through what may be the worst time of their life allows them to progress and to keep moving and growing. Whether it is in your partnership, family, or work situation, let those people know that even though you do not approve or like their behaviour, you value who they are, who they are truly becoming. Being willing to move through your own discomfort and respond to people who are using unlovable behaviour to call for help is the great calling of leadership, and the great test of someone who loves.

Today is a time to be a true leader in your relationship and in your life. Look for ways you can reach new levels of responsiveness, both at home and at work.

An attack is a call for help.

When we are attacked, we tend to put up defences, run away, or attack back. But if we realise the attack is a call for help, and respond with openness and move toward the person, we would enlist this person as one of our greatest supporters. Moving toward an attacker can only be with a certain sense of confidence. When a person attacks, they are going through some of their hardest times. If while you were being attacked, you just poured love into the person attacking you, the next time you were together, you would find you both had moved forward. Your attacker would somehow feel bonded or connected with you, because when someone attacks, they are frightened and do not expect the other person to move toward them. But even if nothing else happened, they feel the love. So attack is a perfect opportunity to establish bonding with the person who's attacking you.

One of the greatest acts of leadership is to realise an attack is a call for help. Be the leader in your relationship today.

141 A role is the costume for an unmourned loss.

The role may be one of dependence in which we act very needy but are unable to receive. Or we may adopt an independent role and act as if we do not care about the loss. (But saying we don't care really hints at how much we do care.) Or, we try to be the helper, helping everyone else with their pain, but always covering up our own, thus becoming the "untrue helper". As such, we limit our capacity to help others. If we do not deal with our losses by experiencing all the feelings, we do not make a new beginning. And somehow, none of the roles helps us move forward.

Take a look at what you have used to move away from your old losses. Are you in a state of dependence, or independence, or in the helping role? What was the loss you have not recovered from? Allow yourself to feel the feelings of loss, not as the adult you are, but as the child inside who still mourns that loss. Allow yourself, as that child, to finish the mourning process. Be willing to move past your roles to find the birth that waits for you.

142 A bad feeling is released by true giving.

When we feel self-conscious or embarrassed or criticised, we tend to contract. But if we gave at the very time we felt bad, we would be expanded. We would know ourselves as bigger by stepping through the wall of our personalities.

Ask yourself, "Who needs my help?" Whoever pops into your mind, ask yourself, "What is the best way for me to help them?" and see what comes into your mind. You could send love by calling, writing, or supporting them in some way. They may need a certain thing, which you could imagine pouring down from the universe, filling you, and pouring through you to them. In reaching out to them, you will find you have broken the invisible wall around you, and will feel good again.

143 Jealousy is revenge on yourself.

It means we have attached our happiness to someone else's behaviour, which will certainly cause us pain. It is one of the most unpleasant feelings we can have – a combination of dependency, neediness, a sense of fear of loss, a feeling of hurt, rejection, unworthiness, valuelessness and anger. It alone is enough to drive a person into independence.

Jealousy is also a form of emotional blackmail; we use it to try to control another person through our bad feelings, whether they know what we feel or not. But it can only occur when you are competing for someone and believe you are the one who is losing. (In fact, all competition is premised on belief in loss.) To release yourself from jealousy, be willing to take your criteria of self-value away from another's actions. They may be doing what they are doing out of their own needs or compulsions.

Today, be willing to let go of your attachment, because as you step forward, the situation will change and unfold. The more you step forward, the more everyone can win by finding their natural relationship. If this is not the person who is truly for you, you will find someone who is. When you have let go and moved forward, you will find much greater peace in your committed relationships, and your attractiveness will come back. This does not mean throwing the person away, or running away from the situation, but letting go of your attachments about how the situation should be.

Find the negative beliefs of loss or competition that led to this situation. By catching yourself in your beliefs and making a new choice, you can change the old ones. While you may have thousands of negative beliefs about relationships each one you choose to change moves things forward in a positive direction.

144 The extent of your jealousy is the extent to which you feel untrustworthy.

So you project onto your partner how you think you might act in a similar situation. This is one of the most hidden things about jealousy. If we were to gain more trust in ourselves, heal our old broken hearts and experience ourselves as more valuable, we would be able to feel more worthy of commitment to ourselves and others. We would give up being so fickle, allow ourselves to receive, and know ourselves as worthy of what we receive.

The extent to which we feel untrustworthy is the extent to which we punish our partner. We punish them and ourselves with our jealousy. The key here is becoming more trustworthy yourself – not more dependent. Begin to value yourself, because valuing yourself allows you to make commitments.

145 Every fantasy is an expectation, and under that, a demand.

A fantasy says, "This is the way it would be if my needs were met." We make a picture to receive some kind of nurturing from a situation in which we are not receiving enough. Yet the more we bring this fantasy into the present situation to feel nurtured, the less exciting the situation becomes. So we keep making our fantasies bigger and bigger to create more and more excitement.

Like expectations, fantasies block receiving. They block the real nurturing your situation could give you. Be willing to let go of your fantasies so you can be open to what is there and enjoy it. Otherwise, fantasy locks you into a certain reality that does not allow you to move forward. If you let go of your fantasies – the castles in the clouds and the pipe dreams – you will find yourself receiving more.

Take a look at how much fantasy is in your life. Look at romance, sex, career, the lottery, and so on. Begin to let go and move closer into the situation, and into closer contact with your partner. The more you get to know your partner and make contact with them, the greater the natural electricity of sexuality in your relationship, and the more the relationship unfolds.

146 The goal of every relationship is interdependence:

Where both people are equally balanced in relation to each other; and where there is a balance within each person of their masculine and feminine sides, which results in a balanced relationship of masculine and feminine energies.

When we move out of the romance stage of our relationship, each partner polarise – one into more independence and the other to more dependence. If you are the independent person in the relationship, your goal is to reach out and value your partner. (Sometimes the power struggle stage in a relationship is primarily the fight for who's going to be the most independent one.) If you are the dependent one, your goal is to let go of your attachments and pain, and feel your true feelings until you move the relationship up to a whole new level of partnership. No matter what position you are in, you can constantly move your relationship ahead.

Take time today to set the goal for your relationship for interdependence. If you do not have a goal, you can end up anywhere, and you can be stopped by anything. Every time you think in any way about your partner, your relationship, or about your experience in the relationship, see the goal of interdependence and balance in your relationship.

147 Your mother and father are embodiments of your feminine and masculine sides.

Sometimes, if your parents are at war, your masculine and feminine will be at war also. If your parents were out of balance, the masculine and feminine within you are likely to be out of balance, too. And if they are out of balance within you, they will be out of balance in your relationship.

As you heal the woman or feminine in you, your mother is healed. As you heal the father or the masculine within you, your father is healed. As you learn the value of the masculine and its ability to give and initiate, as well as the feminine and its ability to receive and nurture, each will naturally come to balance within you.

When you are independent, the feminine within you is wounded. But in learning how to respond to your own needs, you will find yourself with a much greater ability to receive. Thus, your masculine will move out of the independent – or the untrue masculine – and finds its natural initiating stance in the relationship.

Imagine the man and woman in you. Which needs help? If the man in you needs help, let the woman receive Heaven's grace to empower the man. If the woman needs help, let the man go to her and sustain her, protect her, love her, foster her. As you do this, you will find the masculine and feminine within you come to a greater healing balance. This will have an effect both on your parents and on your own relationship.

148 Every old love from the past you are holding on to keeps you from taking the next step in your present relationship.

The mind is a funny thing. If you are fantasising about something, your mind does not know if it is real or just a fantasy, because in the mind it is all an image. So when you are thinking about the good things in an old relationship, the mind says, "Hey. We're satisfied; we already have it. Why create it now?" Your willingness to let go of all the good things from the past that you ever received will allow those things to emerge in your present relationship. What you receive now will be even stronger and more generative than it was in the past.

See who you are holding on to from the past because it is keeping your present relationship from moving to a new level, and keeping you from moving too. Be willing to let go of those old loves. They are great gifts from Heaven, but not gifts to be used to hold back your present happiness. Be willing to receive it all now.

You may find that you are not so much holding on to an old relationship as much as a quality from that relationship. Today be willing to put any of these qualities into the hands of your Higher Mind to let go for you.

149 When you feel overwhelmed by your partner's needs, become a channel for Heaven's grace.

Sometimes we feel too tired, as if there is not enough of us to satisfy our partner, or help them or take care of them. When you do not have the strength to move forward, allow your partnership to move you forward. When you feel burnt out, ask for Heaven's help. If you try to use your own energy, sometimes you feel sucked dry within a few minutes. By tapping into the Universe, you will find enough grace to feed everyone.

Think of someone around you who is needy. Imagine the energy of the Universe pouring through you and filling them up. Imagine this energy is constantly running through you all day for anybody who has needs around you. You will notice that as the energy pours through you to other people, you also are filled.

150 If your relationship feels dead, look for the hidden competition.

Where there is competition, there is separation. Where there is separation, there is a lack of contact, and that creates deadness. All of these feelings really hold you back. So be willing to give up all these areas of subtle competition, and look for a place of cooperation, where you can move together with your partner. When you cooperate, you are naturally moving in harmony with your partner.

Today, take a good look at where you are considering yourself a little bit better or a little bit more right. Ask yourself, "Where am I considering myself the best one, the who deserves to be supported in a better way?" Be willing to look for a place of harmony with your partner instead of the subtle or not so subtle competition that destroys a relationship.

151 All relationships are no-fault relationships.

Recognising this, that no one is to blame and everyone is doing the very best they can given their circumstances, allows us to see our relationships in a true light and to keep progressing in all of them. But any time there is blame, a relationship stops growing and begins to die.

Today, make a decision for all of your relationships to become no fault. The faults you see in the world or others is really the reflection of the hidden or not so hidden faults in yourself. Make a list of all the places where you have blame going towards someone. You will probably find you have some sort of judgement or blame going toward everyone around you. Your willingness to see them and yourself as innocent allows everyone to move forward and receive more.

152 Everything that happens in a relationship has two sources.

Many times we hold grievances against our partners because we believe they did something to us. But if you were to know your subconscious mind, you would realise no one is doing anything to you that you are not already doing to yourself. Everything that happens in a relationship is a form of collusion. When a relationship gets ready to end, at some level both people are choosing its end. At a subconscious level, they are choosing who's going to be the independent one – the bad guy, and who's going to be the dependent one – the one who carries the heartbreak. Both people choose the role they can best use to end the relationship. Everything that happens is the result of choice.

Consider three situations you think you did not want to happen. Now take one of them and imagine for a moment you actually did want it to happen. You know you did not want it consciously, but the reason it happened – given all circumstances – is that a part of you chose it as the very best way. Talk to that part of you. Find out what was going on that led you to make the choice you did. What was the purpose behind the event? What did it allow you to do? What did you not have to do? Just pretend you are that part. Listen to what comes to your mind, and you will find the underlying motivation for your co-creation of that event. Maybe it is time to let all that go and move forward again so you can be happier in your present relationship.

153 The amount of recognition which you receive is the amount to which you recognise yourself.

Other people will mirror your experience of yourself back to you. This is also true of how much you approve of yourself. So if you are not valuing yourself, you are not going to recognise the amount of recognition coming toward you, which is really self-recognition.

Spend time today taking a look at how much approval or recognition you seem to be receiving from the world around you. Spend one day just valuing yourself and giving to yourself.

154 The amount of approval you receive is the amount you give to others.

The extent to which we give approval, friendship or love, is the extent to which these gifts come back to us. When you give by recognising others, you are recognised. When you share your gifts with others, you feel gifted. The extent of approval you are receiving in your life is really the extent to which you are not judging those around you, and therefore naturally giving forth to them. As you give, they naturally respond with their approval, recognition, and love.

If you find any lack of recognition in your life, give it to those around you. Give especially to those from whom you need it the most.

155 Guilt holds back your power.

To the extent you feel guilty you will be withdrawn. If you feel guilty, at some level you feel you are bad, and are afraid to bring yourself forward because your badness might show. So you keep yourself withdrawn, or sometimes you attack. But attack is a form of domination that shows your lack of power and how much you are in fear.

Take any guilt or bad feelings, and place them in the hands of God, where you can only be innocent. Imagine that you are taking your guilt and sending it out on a little boat. As the boat is carried down a swiftly flowing river, the river cleans all of the guilt out of your mind, freeing you so you can step forward. Take a deep breath. Feel all that air coming into your lungs. Feel how much you can receive from life. Feel that you can naturally be yourself – you can express yourself and your power.

156 Any problem outside your relationship can be healed within it.

Everything outside your relationship can be seen as a metaphor or mirror for something happening in the mind and heart of your relationship; it points to a place within your relationship that is yet to be connected. If scarcity surrounds you, there is scarcity within your relationship. This means it is time to give and receive truly – not just in sacrifice and burn out. As you connect and find new joy within your relationship, you will reach a new level of partnership and co-creativity. Correspondingly, you will find the outside problem begins to heal. One of the deepest and most powerful secrets about a relationship is this power to heal whatever problems surround you, no matter what their depths.

Choose a problem, maybe one your partner and you would like to work on together. Now imagine the problem is somehow between your partner and you. Sometimes you will even be able to find the area in your relationship that has not yet been connected. When you move to connect in this way, you will find creativity flowing through you and your relationship, and out to heal the world.

157 In your relationship you can choose drama or you can choose creativity.

The drama gets created for two reasons. Either you are in a power struggle, and one, or both of you, find increasingly dramatic ways to express your point; or the relationship seems dull, so you create drama to relieve deadness. But every power struggle and every form of deadness in your relationship is just an avoidance of your creativity.

Concentrate on an area in your relationship either where you are in conflict or there is a sense of deadness. Imagine you are floating down past it into a deeper layer. In that deeper layer, come to a place where there is something creative you are being called to do, something that would really help you feel fulfilled. Feel the energy juicing inside you and rushing out to be expressed. This creativity is your life. It energises you and helps you to feel the love that is really you.

158 The helper role comes from believing you are destructive.

In the psychodynamics of everyone who has felt compelled to adopt a healing role is a belief that long ago we were guilty of causing some kind of pain, or that we could not help at a time of great need. Although belief in your guilt is a misunderstanding, the child within doesn't know that. As children, we tend to blame ourselves for the destructiveness, illness and death around us. So, later on we take on the role of healer.

Now all of us at some point take on this role, but it comes out of our own guilt. That is why sometimes you can help ninety-nine people, but if you miss one, you feel as guilty as if you had missed them all. This is a sure sign you are in the role of the helper, the enabler or the untrue helper. These roles compensate for feelings of guilt, wrongness or destructiveness, and it stops you from receiving.

Taking a giant step forward as a helper to become the healed healer and to finally receive allows you to have the strength and the vision to help a great many more people than you are presently helping. It allows you to move out of roles in your relationship, to be more responsive to your partner, and to receive more love and gratitude from your partner and the world.

Look at the helping roles you are playing, and ask yourself, "Where did I begin to believe it was my fault? that I was helpless? that I was destructive?" Take your adult mind back to those childhood places and look at them again. See if you can keep from condemning yourself for what occurred. Realise that what you blamed yourself for, you have come to be the antidote of – but you can only do that from your centre which you left so long ago. Ask your Higher Power to carry you back to your centre, and from there radiate what is needed to all those around you. It will come from your being who you are – not what you do. Let go of the past. Find the vision and love that wants to express itself through who you are.

159 Appreciation is one of the easiest ways to heal anything.

Any pain, problem, or wound is a place where somehow we have stopped. Appreciation begins that healing process that moves you into the flow. If abundance or anything seems stuck, begin the flow again. All day long appreciate as many people as you can; the world around you; the breath you are taking in right now; the senses you have been given to enjoy.

If there is a problem between your partner and you, keep telling them everything you appreciate about them until the problem between you melts away in your warmth. No problem can withstand the power of appreciation.

160 The purpose of every enemy is to bring back a long-buried piece of your mind

– a piece of you that you lost long ago. The force that your enemy brings against you is an energy that can always be used for your healing; at a deep level of your mind, it actually reflects the amount of your own energy that you are using against yourself. If you do not resist the energy and allow it to move into you, you can leap up to a higher level of consciousness. The first step is to appreciate your enemy and what they are showing you. Your willingness to forgive and trust in that can bring the split part of you back into full integration.

Take a look at your enemy. What quality or qualities are you fighting against? Have you ever acted in that way? If you cannot remember, was there anyone close to you who did act that way? What would you – or anyone – have to be feeling to behave in such a fashion? If you cannot identify with this feeling, then ask yourself, what is the feeling underneath it that drove the behaviour? When you finally get to a feeling you can identify with, allow that to be the bridge of compassion and commonality that joins you to the person who had been your enemy. The more you use that bridge, the more you understand and find a common purpose.

161 Most conflicts are healed by clarifying your experience.

Every conflict is a form of misunderstanding. To resolve the conflict, explain your experience to your partner and listen carefully to their experience and what they were feeling to act the way they did. As you fully understand your partner's experience, and as they fully understand yours, you will find you are naturally joining together and moving forward.

Today, in any situation which you feel is not completely resolved, where there are any misunderstandings, begin to talk about what is going on for you. See what is going on for your partner, too – what the meaning is for them, why they are acting and feeling the way they are. Do not forget to reaffirm your partner and the value of your relationship in this conflict. Clarification of your feelings and the other person's will deal with about eighty-five percent of all conflicts.

162 If you don't have a relationship, it's because you have closed the door.

At the end of a relationship, we sometimes do this because of the pain and anger we experience. Then we completely repress that we have shut the door on all relationships. After a certain amount of time, we go out looking for new relationships, but no matter how long, or how hard, or in how many directions we look, we cannot seem to find anyone eligible who interests us. This is because we have shut the door. The good news is, you can fling the door wide open and begin again right now.

If you are already in a relationship, you might take a look at what seems to be missing in it. When did you close the door to that particular quality? Why did you shut the door? Imagine you are swinging the door wide open. As soon as you do, what you are missing will come your way.

163 The truth always helps.

If you are in a dead or conflicted situation, and you do not know what could help, the truth will move you forward by pulling you out of withdrawal. Truth is a form of giving. What truth are you not telling? What truth are you holding back from your partner or the situation around you? That truth is vital now. It will set you free. Do not just unload on your partner. You would do that only if you weren't telling the truth about deeper feelings.

Get yourself out of prison. Go tell the truth.

164 Keep telling the truth until everyone wins.

Truth is not a weapon with which to bludgeon the people around you. It allows everyone to win. Truth is the integration of all perspectives in the present situation. When this happens, everyone is motivated to move forward. So, unless everyone wins around you, it is not the final truth.

Keep communicating until everyone feels as if they have won, and everything is resolved. What always hurts is a situation in which people have not told enough of the truth to come to full understanding and resolution. Do not stop at compromise, because then you will feel as if you are in sacrifice, and everyone will feel as if they are losing. The truth means everybody wins.

165 The only problem is separation, and love heals separation.

If you followed every problem down to its most basic dynamic, at the very bottom you would find fear and separation. So whatever the problem is, the solution is simple – love. Heal the separation. Make the bridge. Create the bonding. Whether the symptom is guilt, fear, or sickness – any form of conflict that causes us to feel separate – use love, forgiveness, and bonding. This is the glue to make everything come together and the problem disappear.

Choose two of your greatest problems, and look for the place of separation. Give love as the way of healing the separation, and when it is healed, the problem will disappear. Practice love as the answer.

Commitment allows for greater self-expression.

It creates safety, freedom, and ease, through which you have a greater opportunity to find your gifts and to express them. Once a person feels they have the kind of safety net a committed relationship provides, they go on to find greater creativity and higher levels of self-expression within themselves.

Today, value your partner for the new things that have developed in you since your relationship began. Appreciate your partner for what they have given you. Tell your partner that as a result of the commitment in your relationship, these new aspects of yourself have had a chance to grow.

167 A broken heart is really a broken expectation that another would fill your needs.

You cannot have a broken heart if you are willing to let go of your expectations and your rules about how your partner should be. When you let go of your expectations, you have a certain flexibility.

Take a look at where you may be experiencing some form of heartbreak, or where you are still suffering from an old heartbreak. Realise this was your unspoken demand for the relationship to unfold according to your rules, and for the person to act according to your needs. Be willing to let all of that go so you can move forward and receive. This will allow you to feel the love you have been missing.

168 If you are attracted to a person, you have a gift for them.

Often, when we are attracted to somebody, we think they are supposed to give us something. But your joy comes in realising that if you give the gift, a creative project will come to both of you as a result of that connection. If you willingly give your gift with integrity, you will enjoy a creative connection with many joyful people.

See who you feel attracted to in your surrounding area, and ask yourself, "What is the gift I am to give to them that would really move them forward?" Maybe it is just a blessing or a feeling of support. Give your gift with integrity and love, and without any expectation in return.

169 If you give up being right, you can be happy.

Being right closes the situation and does not allow any new information to come in. If you look at where you are being right, that is where you have stopped the unfolding by your own choice. Being right is actually a way of hiding how wrong you feel inside. You can be right, or you can be happy, but you cannot be both.

Write down the areas where you are stuck and not receiving in your life. Next to each area, write down all the ways you are being right about that situation. Be willing to let these go, and let new answers come to light. Give up this futile defence you use to hide your guilt, and be willing to allow yourself to be happy.

170 The role gets the reward, while you remain in sacrifice.

A role is a place where you give but cannot receive. The role reaps the reward, and you get the feelings of tiredness and burn-out. But whatever you are trying to prove by this role is probably already true about you – so why do you need to prove it?

Allow yourself to receive the reward for all of your work; enjoy your partner, your family, your work, your life, the air you breathe, the food you eat, and everything you do. Enjoy the natural good feeling that comes from giving. Make the choice to do the right thing, but for the right reason – because you choose to, not because you are supposed to. What you choose becomes your commitment.

Look at any area where you do not seem to be receiving or getting anything out of what you are doing. See whether you are in a role, or naturally giving out of your own choice. By choosing to do the right thing, you can totally correct any situation, no matter how difficult. Your choice will empower you and give you energy.

171 If separation is at the heart of every problem, then all healing comes from joining.

Move toward people, and the situation will begin to move forward. Just go in and establish rapport. As you create intimacy, you will find the point of natural bonding in the relationship. Overcome or overlook the little things that seem to come up, and you will find the natural joining.

So today, choose one big, juicy problem. Who are the key people in that situation? Move toward them in any way until you feel as if you have joined them. Whatever it takes to join them – communication, forgiveness, moving off your "position" – it will be worth it. You may not agree with everything they are saying, but you will feel personally close to them and then a new answer will come through for both of you.

172 Every birth feels like a death.

If you woke up in the middle of the night, and you were being born, you would feel as if you were dying. In situations that seem to be closing in around you, realise that as one aspect of your life closes, another one begins. Be willing to let go so this new birth can occur.

Take a look at your life, and see if a situation seems to be ending, or if something seems to be closing down. Realise what needs to finish so the new beginning can occur. It is happening so you can find a new life on the ashes of the old. A new chapter is about to begin. Do not miss it because you mistook the end of the chapter as the end of it all. If you trust what seems like death, it will become your birth.

173 You have the resources to meet the needs of every situation.

Every situation you face comes to you at that point because you are able to transcend the situation and come up with the healing answer that could assist everyone. There is a place in your mind that knows the answer, however paradoxical, to all your major conflicts. When you are ready for the next lesson, that lesson appears.

Choose a problem area in your life that seems beyond you. Ask your Higher Power to take over and handle it. Over the next twenty-four hours, just watch what seems to occur in the situation. Get out of the way, and trust that as the situation unfolds, either the entire problem will be solved, or the next layer. If just a layer is solved, keep asking for help until every layer of the entire problem is healed.

174 **You can experience guilt only if you are using someone or something to hold yourself back.**

The purpose of guilt is to protect you from the fear you might feel if you moved forward. When you realise this, you can look again at situations where you have felt guilty and make the choice to move forward in your life.

What are you still feeling guilty about? How are you using guilt to hold yourself back? Maybe at a certain point in your life you did not feel you could handle a particular gift or ability or aspect of yourself. Now you have the maturity and the wisdom to do that. Choose to move forward in your life.

175 You are responsible for your own feelings, because they are coming from inside of you.

Nobody can make you feel what is not within you. If you say somebody makes you feel angry or hurt, you are saying that they can get inside you and grab your anger throttle or push your hurt button. It is not true. You have a choice about what you feel. Often it is a split-second choice, because most of us are reactive to outside situations. If there is pain inside us, situations will arise that naturally trigger it forth.

If we try to make someone else responsible for our feelings, we belittle and victimise ourselves. If we believe someone else is responsible for our feelings, we then have to manipulate them to do things differently so we can feel good. But if we are responsible for our own feelings, then we can change them.

Take responsibility for your feelings, and you will take all forms of manipulation and emotional blackmail out of the situation. Your negative feelings point to a lesson you need to learn, something you are called upon to change, or something that wants to be healed. You can change your feelings.

176 Fear is attraction.

Psychological tests have shown that as fear increases, so does sexual energy. At a deeper level, we are afraid of that to which we are also attracted: if you are afraid of death, at some level you are flirting with death; if you are afraid of something happening to your partner, at some level there is a desire for it to happen. This is one of the most hidden parts of your mind, and it is natural to repress it. Fear creates just as love and hate create.

Take a look at what you fear. What is your hidden attraction to it? Examine your fear as something you would like to happen. Bring the fear into the light, and see what you really do want. Know that bringing what is in the darkness of your mind into the light creates healing.

177 The extent of your openness is the extent to which you inspire others.

Many of us are afraid to reveal ourselves, or we show just the nice things about ourselves. If we were to share our real feelings – including the places where we are afraid, ashamed or feel bad – we would find that our integrity would inspire others and move them toward us; it would also allow us to make contact with them. It is a paradox that we hold back this side of ourselves so that people will like us, when sharing it would make us real and accessible.

Today, get real and share what you are experiencing. Do not homogenise it, pasteurise it, or wrap it up in "nice" cellophane. Do not share to manipulate or change anyone. Share to change yourself and to reach out, and the people around you will feel inspired to move forward.

178

To clear up a problem in your career, forgive your father.

Many of us feel unsupported, unrecognised, misunderstood by our father, as if we have been attacked by him. But we can feel our father's competition only if we are competing. We can see our father's failure only if at a very deep level, we have wished our father to fail. As we give forth to our fathers, we find that all our authority figures are seen in a new light. As we forgive our fathers, we find that we move forward in our careers. Your father, your masculine side, and your work are all interrelated.

Take a new look at your father. What you give to him spells your success. Even though he may have died, you can still give to him and forgive him. As you give to him, the father in you increases, and wherever your father is, he will feel blessed by your understanding.

179 Relationships help bond all the fractured pieces.

All lessons that we failed to learn created fractured pieces. Every time we were crushed or traumatised we actually had an opportunity to step into a much higher level of love, understanding, and bonding. Our relationships recreate that opportunity because through them all of those tests will be presented to us again. They are the workshop in which we can relearn the lesson.

Look at any conflict situation, and realise it is an opportunity to retake a test that you failed the first time. Although, sometimes, unlearned lessons become trials when they are presented to us again, you can now pass this trial. Ask for Heaven's help, respond to the situation with as much communication and responsiveness as possible, apologise if necessary, and find yourself having learned the lesson and moving forward.

180 Everyone who comes to you for help is coming to save you.

They come to help you heal a piece of yourself that you ordinarily would not know is wounded or incomplete. Many times, when we have healed something on the surface, something within us is unfinished. Then we discover the advice we give is the very thing we most need to hear.

Be especially grateful today to anyone who comes to you for help. Be responsive to them, realising they are actually bringing back a missing piece of yourself, a piece that will lead you to a new level of success. Listen to your own advice, and the situation will be saved for all.

181 What you reject in your parents is an unlearned lesson your partner will act out.

Your parents have represented your inner world, your subconscious mind. They are projections of two of the most vital parts of your mind available for healing. You have projected onto your parents, and now your partner, parts of yourself you did not like. But what you reject will continue to plague you until you can forgive or integrate it, so the judgement and the self-judgement fall away.

Today is the day to learn this lesson. Ask for help, open your mind, be a little bit more responsive, hold back your judgements, feel your heart flowing out to meet your partner, and let the mask you have made them wear fall away. As you do this, you will find you are not willing to hold against yourself what you have held against your parents and your partner. Everyone will be free.

182 When a problem in your relationship feels beyond you, ask for Heaven's help to heal it.

We have all had problems that felt beyond us, or conflicts so painful we have felt without the resources, or the strength or the courage to face them. This is the time to ask for Heaven's help. As you learn to partner, you will also learn to partner with your creativity and Heaven.

Be willing to receive from Heaven, no matter how big the problem looks. This is the time to open your heart and receive the grace that would move you and your partner forward.

183 **If you want the best in your relationship, give the relationship your best.**

What you give in your relationship allows you to recognise what you are receiving. Giving the best of yourself allows you to enjoy the best in other people. It opens doors that otherwise would not be opened and provides the opportunities for new gifts, new fun, and new enjoyment to arise in your relationship.

Today, give your very best. Give your heart, your all, and notice what a great day it is.

184 Pain is the energy needed to hold on to a negative thought about yourself.

If you are willing to release your pain, the negative thought or self-concept about yourself will also naturally shift. Your willingness to experience the pain until it is gone will free the energy constricting you. Conversely, letting go of negative self-concepts will release pain for you easily.

Today, be willing to let go of your pain. Realise you have been using the negative thought or self-concept to keep you from moving forward, because you have been afraid to face something that will make you much happier. As you let go, you will find a new capacity to receive and enjoy yourself.

185 What you resist in another is what you resist in yourself.

That is, what is in your subconscious mind: part of you is resisting another part of you that you have judged and buried. If you were willing to stop resisting this part of yourself and understand it, the other person would seem to change before your eyes, and you would find yourselves moving forward together.

Acknowledge this part as yours, and feel it totally inside you until your discomfort moves to acceptance. At that point, you will feel free, and the other person will be freed also.

186 The happiness that comes from within cannot be lost.

When we depend on outer things for our happiness, we can lose it when those things change. But if you are giving love and happiness from within, even in difficult situations, you will be healing and growing immensely and you will find your joy is increased.

Look at any situation where your happiness seems to be dependent on outside things. With a little shift, give that happiness from within you. If you are generating happiness, everyone will get the benefit, everyone will be nurtured, and everyone will get to move forward.

187 If anything you are doing is hard work, you are stuck in a role.

– and it is not working. A role sets out to prove how good and virtuous you are. You work extra hard and find yourself explaining how "tough it was, but how you got through it" just to win some admiration. But by trying to do it all yourself, you are relying too much on your own independence. And this is just a way of holding things back. Let go of the guilt, and the difficulty will fall away. You do not have to prove anything any more. In your essence you are truly good.

In situations that seem difficult, allow Heaven to move its grace through you and into the situation. Let the people around you help you. Everything will be so much easier. Give what you are called to give, but remember, you are a much more vital resource when you are not doing the work of a drone. The power and openness of your mind can bring in a grace and resourcefulness that frees everyone.

188 The biggest secret of an independent person is that they have not let go of someone from the past.

At some level of your mind you are still attached to a person from the past, perhaps because you experienced a heartbreak. Your rejection of this negative experience is keeping you independent and blocking you from moving on toward interdependence and the joys of a relationship that is alive and well in the present. Or you may be fantasising about recreating a positive part of your past or having a particular person turn up at your doorstep. But holding on to the past keeps the positive aspects of your fantasy from occurring in your present situation.

Today, let go of the people to whom you are positively or negatively attached. As you are willing to let them go, you will find new opportunities for the return of the feelings you had lost. The fear and loss will disappear and you will begin to feel that good things are coming your way.

189 All pain comes from attachment.

When we lose what we are attached to, we suffer. But what was truly connected can never be disconnected, and the love we have given can never be lost. Our willingness to let go of our attachments is the key element in keeping us out of pain. Our willingness to keep connecting – rather than attaching – allows us to enjoy the people we are with and the circumstances we are in without feeling pain as they change or as the situation moves forward.

In every place where you are suffering, ask yourself, "To what am I attached"? Be willing to let that go. Where you may be attached now is a place of present or future suffering. If you are willing to let go of that, you will feel yourself moving forward. Without attachment the pain is taken out of your experience, and you can receive and enjoy.

If it hurts it isn't love.

In spite of what all the songs, books and movies tell you, love does not hurt. What hurts is not getting your needs met ... or not getting what you want ... or when something in a relationship brings up the old pain. Love cannot hurt because it is a feeling of contact that brings joy. But when you contract or pull away, that hurts.

Sometimes when your heart expands, it feels a bit like hurt. But that is poignancy, the richness of your heart growing in love and appreciation. It is your heart beginning to dance again after it has been crippled a long time. There is a real sweetness to that feeling.

Look at the situations where you have tried to measure your love by your hurt. Many of us have disguised our needs as love, and then tried to get the other person to respond. Be willing to let go of these needs so you can move forward to make contact with your partner – not as you want them to be but as they really are.

191 The less you defend yourself, the safer you are.

In other words, the extent to which you stand undefended, is the extent to which you will eventually succeed. Conversely, the more defensive you are, the more you create attack. Remember, our defences arise to protect buried pain from the past, but that pain poisons us. If you are aware of this, an attack will help in your healing.

If you are attacked, do not be afraid to feel your feelings. Openness is the heart of communication. It is the ability to give and to be yourself without excuse. The truth does not need defending. Only our ego, the hider of all pain and the essence of separation, needs defence. By remaining undefended, another gift is given to you – the support of those around you.

Stand as undefended as possible to everything moving toward you. Everything today will serve as your teacher. Openness allows teaching to come in the gentlest possible way.

192 Fear is almost excitement.

If you pay attention to fear, you will notice it is energy trying to move through your body. Your fear is a resistance to the energy coming through you as excitement. Yet, we spend millions of dollars every year trying almost anything to create excitement in our life – we jump out of aeroplanes, climb mountains, go to horror movies and so on.

All we have to do is look at what is frightening us, stop resisting it, and let that energy provide a thrill.

Today, spend some time looking at what you are afraid of. See where the energy is trapped in your body, and be willing to let it move up through your body until it overflows from the top of your head. This could be a most exciting day!

193 **Loss is the first step to a new beginning.**

Loss comes to teach us that what we were attached to could not really sustain us. We are being asked to grow, mature, and move on. But if we do not finish our mourning, if we hold on to the past, if we go into depressions so as not to move forward, then we do not have our new beginning. We do not see the dawn coming up after the dark if we resist the night.

Loss is really about a new beginning. Be willing to let go of your losses so the new birth will show itself, and the next good thing can come to you.

194 Hurt can be changed to tenderness.

If we do not resist the feeling of hurt, and move into contraction, then we can experience a great feeling of tenderness. Unresisted hurt creates an opening in our heart where old pain can come forth and be healed. So do not resist.

Today, let the lips of your wounds sing the songs of your heart.

195 Guilt is blocked wisdom in that we use it to remove ourselves from the lesson to be learned.

(And every lesson is there to be learned). So we attack and punish ourselves to pay for the mistake. This stops us and keeps us stuck. But what if every time we made a mistake as children we had begun to punish ourselves? ... We would never have learned how to walk.

Guilt is almost wisdom, but until the lesson is learned, it is a form of punishing yourself for not making a simple correction. Our willingness to learn the lesson corrects the mistake, which adds to our knowledge and wisdom.

Look at the area of your guilt, and be willing to see the lesson life wants you to learn so you will be released into greater wisdom.

196 Sacrifice is the role of love.

While sacrifice contains a desire to give, it leaves out one very important element – you. Because sacrifice is played out through a role without your really giving yourself, it gives, but cannot really receive. So it cheats your partner out of the value of your gift, because if you devalue yourself there is nothing of worth for them to receive. And your partner is also cheated out of their ability to give back to you.

Valuing yourself allows sacrifice to be transformed to love, not counterfeit love. And giving yourself in what you give is the greatest gift of all because it allows you to receive – which means there will always be more to give.

Look at the areas where you are in sacrifice, and realise that part of you is being withheld. Today, fully give yourself so you can fully receive all the love that is meant for you.

197 Disappointment signals a need for release.

Most of us stop at the first stage of disappointment because things have not turned out the way we felt we needed them to. But if we were willing to experience the disappointment and the need within it, and then let it go, we would be moved out of stress into success. We would listen to life's rhythms rather than trying to squeeze life into our concepts. If we can let go, we can be taught that our disappointment lets us know our picture of life was not a true one. We can become like an empty glass that can be filled with what life is really about, rather than filled glasses that cannot take in anything more.

Today, empty your glass of all disappointments and stand open to what life will teach you.

Frustration is a lack of understanding.

It means we have been disappointed that our expectations have not been met, that things have not turned out our way – which of course we consider the right way, the best way. If we were willing to move past our frustration, we would reach a full understanding. There is something about our partner, or our situation or ourselves we do not fully understand. Begin with understanding, complete the cycle, unlock the prison of frustration, and you will move forward together.

In areas where you feel frustrated, ask for a deeper awareness that could be teaching you. All awareness creates a flow and moves you forward. Your understanding is the key today.

199 It is impossible to feel fear in the present moment.

Trying to live in the future means you expect the future to be like the past. And trying to live the future now – which is impossible – creates strain and fear in the present. In fact, if you move five minutes ahead in a very difficult situation, you can create a lot of fear. But if you live fully in the present moment, no matter how difficult it is, it would be so different that it would change your future, and the fear would disappear. This moment would be a moment of release, of giving. Being fully here, in this moment, opens the door to eternity and love, which is the opposite of fear.

Look at way you are creating fear for yourself by living in the future. The future will take care of itself. Place your future in the hands of God, and live today so you may enjoy it fully. Live so you may receive the richness and nectar of each moment.

200 Being a victim is a form of attack.

All of us have been victims at times. Typically, these are the most painful, traumatic times of our life because they seem to come from a situation where we are surprised or even blind-sided. But more is going on in a victim situation than meets the eye, as there is as much violence in a victim as there is in a victimiser: a victimiser sends the violence outward, while the victim directs the violence firstly against themselves, and secondly toward someone else. Every time we are victimised, we attack some person who is significant to us. They may be people who died long ago, but typically they are those who are around us now.

Being a victim is a form of unawareness and a way of being angry. To take it to its deepest metaphysical level, it is a form of attack that says, "I'll show you, God. I'll show you that you are not such a good God. I'll suffer and be unhappy here on your earth." But if we were willing to receive, we would be surrounded by abundance, love and support.

Sit down and write out ten major times you have been a victim. Next to that, write down who you were attacking, and then what you were attacking them for as a natural part of your power struggle. If you have kept who you were attacking a secret from yourself, then an element of the attack is still going on, and is holding you back. Make a choice about whether or not you want the attack to continue.

201 Trust is the mender of old heartbreaks.

In any frightening situation or where there is a problem, trust can heal anything. It is the most important element of confidence. When we trust, we use the power of our mind to choose that everything will turn out for the very best. Trust knows that the dark or painful elements will be transformed, and recognises that sometimes these elements are actually helpful in the long run. Trust heals dissociation, it returns feeling, and allows us tenderness and safety in our relationships.

But do not confuse trust with controlling the outcome, or the process of how the answer will come about. This is not your job. Yet, trust is not naive – that usually leads to heartbreak. When doubts or pain creep in, make the choice that will bring you peace. Trust is the recognition of how powerful you are in any situation. Trust is the power of your mind accepting what is and then transforming through your own mind.

Today is a day of trust. So look at what needs transforming, and bring in the power of your mind, knowing no matter how the situation looks, trust will make it work for you.

All heartbreak hides competition.

Heartbreak is a way of trying to take something from your partner. And you cannot be heartbroken when you are giving, unless you are giving to take. When we compete with our partner to get our needs met, one or both of us begin to act in very independent ways. When they do something against us, we withdraw, attack or ambush. This continual competition creates greater and greater pain until, finally, somebody has a heartbreak.

If you are willing to look at how you and your partner are secretly, or not so secretly, competing, you can begin to shift these power struggles so you both win and get your needs met. This can happen through dialogue in any situation that is difficult. Fully giving yourself, and letting go creates places of major birth for yourself.

Look at areas where you may be competing with your partner. Today, truly give to your partner so you might really enjoy them and know the joys and safety of partnership.

203 All sabotage hides a fear of greater sacrifice.

Sabotage occurs just at a point where we are about to step into a whole new level of success – but at costs in sacrifice too great for us. While everyone else may see us as successful, we are feeling the costs. So to us, success just means a much greater level of sacrifice. We feel we just cannot do it any longer, we cannot take on any more than we already have. So we blow up that future successful situation.

Your willingness to give up sacrifice and to deal yourself into the game, to make more room for yourself to breathe and enjoy life allows a greater courage to step into the future and succeed at a new level.

Today, let go of sacrifice, because that is the only roadblock on your way to a much higher level of success in your relationship and in your career.

204 Dependence in the present points to judgement in the past.

Wherever we are dependent, we have judgement. We think someone or the situation should have, but did not, meet our needs. So to get our needs met in the present situation, we become dependent, thinking, "Surely someone will meet my needs". But dependence simply creates a bad feeling which becomes a vicious circle of, "I'm needy, I feel bad about myself, I feel even more needy, I feel even worse about myself ... and so on." And too, where we have judgement in the past, we also have guilt. Feeling guilty is tied in with needs, which arise from lack of bonding, loss or fear.

It is time to let go of those judgements about how things or someone should have been. Be willing to forgive the past and more openly embrace the next step and you will find that your needs will naturally be met.

205 Every relationship is a reflection of your relationship to yourself.

If someone is mistreating or abusing you, it is only because you are mistreating or abusing yourself. If someone is raping you, how are you forcing yourself? Take a deep look at your life. If people are not respecting you, what is it about you that does not ask for respect? If you do not like your relationships, change how you are treating yourself. People can only be punishing you if at some level you feel guilty and deserve to be punished – that is a mistake.

Today, look at how you are treating yourself. Take ten of your most significant relationships and ask yourself what the key quality is in their treatment of you? Then take a look at how you treat yourself. If you see a negative aspect there, explore where that might have begun. ... With the knowledge you have now, how would you choose to change what you decided in the past, or how you acted then, that helped shape this self-concept? It is only what you are worth to yourself that the world around you will recognise. And you deserve the very best.

Grievances destroy relationships

All grievances do harm. Yet many of us do not want to share our grievances with our partner. This is because we do not want to have to deal with the mess and the pain. But the more you hold on to a grievance, the more you hold yourself back, and the bigger the wall grows between you and your partner. If you are experiencing an area of deadness in your relationship, try sharing your grievances. What grievances do you have, and which of those have you been holding onto from the beginning of your relationship?

Today is a day of communication, of new motivation to not let the backlog of grievances weigh you down and wear you out. Begin by taking down the wall of grievances between both of you, one by one, and find who your partner really is. In truth, no grievance is true – it only serves to make you righteous and unwilling to move forward. Today, be willing to move yourself and your relationship forward.

207 Every trauma offers a choice.

Most of us have had traumatic things happen to us. And when they do, we have a choice as to what the experience will become for us: it may become the thing that wounds us so mortally it will eventually kill us because we have not gotten over it; or, it may become the grain of sand around which we produce a great pearl.

A gift is hidden in every trauma, but it takes a deeper vision to see it. If you have not received the gift, the trauma itself will have become part of your defences, part of the character armour you use to keep pain away. Your willingness to see the gifts with new eyes will allow you to take down the armour and let energy flow that can then be used for your health, vitality, happiness and fun. You will see that, in terms of the healing that needs to be done, everything works for the very best.

Before any trauma comes about you can choose either, the control a trauma brings to you – over yourself and maybe others; or, you can choose to let go of another layer of control, and trust this gift in yourself.

Imagine you are taking one of the traumas you have experienced and are putting it in the Hands of God. Imagine as you do so, a gift comes to you from the heavens. Feel it really coming into you. As you allow yourself to accept this gift, this peace, this new understanding, you will feel your whole life growing again where it had closed down.

208

The role of the lover limits intimacy, because love comes out of spontaneity.

It comes out of your willingness to be born every day once again, to no longer follow the recipes, or go by rote, but to let love teach you and unfold you. When you go by a recipe, you are just acting out how you think a lover should be. At some level, this role hides unworthiness and prevents receiving. Acting out the role can stop you from really being in the fire of love, which can melt you down, heal and purify you, show you the way, take you into ecstasy and into the flow, where you will be more yourself than you have ever been.

Look at the things you do just because you are supposed to do them. Take the oldness and tiredness out of your love situation and do something new. Surprise your partner. Let them really feel love. Today, give them something that is essentially you, which they will always remember.

209 Deadness in sex or your relationship can be healed by moving into a place of birth.

Deadness is a defence to protect yourself from your unconscious mind. One of the fastest ways to move out of deadness is to find the major feeling hiding underneath it. If seen correctly, the feeling has such strength and power that it would automatically move you into a new birth. These feelings are the kind that knock you to your knees – heartbreak, jealousy, terror, violence, anger, emptiness, nothingness, futility – all of these are truly birth situations.

To get out of deadness, ask for the birth situation that the deadness hides. When you hit that place, remember you have asked for this birth, because it is typically a place where there is so much pain that you lose your awareness. This is a place of sacred fire pain, a place of purification.

And all you have to do to move you out of this place, and into the birth process, is to give. Typically, at this point, you are in so much pain you may forget this, or you may feel resistance. Just remember that your giving creates an easy birth. It may be the simplest type of giving – sending love to someone, supporting someone, helping someone in the simplest possible way. The new birth will contain things like a much greater love, a higher level of sexuality, passion, creativity, art, a new level of psychic ability, a new sense of vitality in health, new confidence, power, a greater sense of peace, vision, and purpose.

210 Depression is the fear that something new will leave you.

It is not so much a loss from the past – we have all experienced that. In fact depression is both a loss from the past, and a fear of moving forward. It is the fear that the loss will happen again. So we refuse to go on, or to trust the present or future. We refuse to put our faith into anything because we are afraid our faith will be broken once again, and we will lose something very important.

Today, recognise your depression hides a place of birth. It is time to let go of your past losses and claim the faith to move forward, trusting that life has something better to bring to you. Once you let go, you will find that new birth is waiting for you. Move into a whole new resurrection in your life.

211 Expectations give you no rest, because no matter what the situation is, we are not satisfied.

This actually reflects our dissatisfaction with ourselves, and our feelings of inadequacy.

Expectations are related to perfectionism. To a perfectionist, anything less than perfect is failure. In which case, you have never allowed yourself a reward for what you do. When you complete a job, instead of enjoying a time or place of rest and reward, perfectionism drives you on to the next thing. Because you do not have a rest, you do not have the vision to see a much higher perspective. So you keep making little changes instead of seeing what the next giant leap for you is. You are always worrying, always doing every last little thing, always trying too hard and doing too much.

Then again, some perfectionists never try at all. They think that if they cannot do it perfectly, why even begin? But even if you do nothing at all, in your mind, you are still under so much stress and pressure that you do not have rest within yourself.

Today, let yourself come to reward. Allow yourself the rest that would give a much higher perspective and the celebration that would motivate you to move to the next level. Let go of all your expectations and find the ease of life carrying you forward.

212 Irresistibility is one of the best gifts you can give your partner.

It is feeling your attractiveness to such an extent that your charisma draws the people around you toward you. This is one of the gifts or acts of leadership. As you draw people to you with integrity, you can then lead them forward. It is also a great gift you could give your partner as a way of inspiring them. Irresistibility makes any job go easier. It is full of playfulness and knows that no matter what, you will be loved.

Today, practice your irresistibility, which is really an inner knowing. It is an energy you provide to the world around you. And people love attractiveness because it moves them toward something. As you draw your partner irresistibly toward you, you are offering a gift to yourself as well as to them.

213 **The pain of rejection in our present relationship is to help heal the pain we carry inside ourselves, which is the pain of old heartbreaks.**

In fact we experience the pain of rejection in our relationships to trigger off this old pain. And these heartbreaks we had as children or in our beginning relationships will interfere in our present relationship until they are healed.

So if we are willing just to experience the hurt and realise this is really old pain, and if we can be in touch with what the old pain is and share that, we correspondingly create a certain responsiveness in our partner. Our willingness to communicate about where the pain is coming from frees us and opens.

As you dwell on a present hurt in your life, see if you can find its root. Go back to the situation and imagine heaven pouring through you to meet everybody's needs back there. With the courage of heaven pouring through you, give love to everyone there. Notice how everything in the situation changes, and how you are freed in a very easy way from having to go through all the pain.

214 Your sexual desire may be a cover for your pain, and a great defence.

So by enticing our partner into having sex with us, we do not have to deal with all the pain. But sometimes, when we have the type of sexual desire that is hiding pain, our partner does not seem interested, or is busy, or just does not feel like it. This is the time to take a look at what the sexual energy might be hiding. And letting go of pain always wins back your attractiveness.

If you do not seem to be requited at this moment, take a look at what your desire might be hiding. Your willingness to feel the pain or the feelings underneath your sexual desire, to feel them all the way through until they are finished would motivate your partner to move toward you. Your willingness to burn through your feelings can create great success where you most want it.

215 Commitment means you know there is time for the broken things to heal.

When you are committed, you are in for the long haul. You have set a goal of joint purpose and mutual growth together, and the coming of wholeness for both of you in the relationship. This means you do not run away from conflicts or broken feelings, but that you move forward to heal these things. Commitment means not worrying that every little conflict may be your last. You acknowledge conflicts as they arise, but just as you move through them on the way to finding greater happiness and deeper love.

Close your eyes, and reaffirm the goal in your relationship. What do you want to occur? What do you want with your partner? If any problems confront you now, feel yourself moving naturally through those problems and on to that higher goal. Feel the energy of your partner beside you as you move through each block and step over each hurdle on the way toward this final goal. This is a growth of your own maturity and a realisation of wholeness and greatness. This is a growth of love and beauty in your life.

216 Deadness in a relationship can be healed through giving.

Deadness in your relationship means you are stuck, tired, that you have been in sacrifice. But true giving moves you forward and allows you to receive. Make a choice here. How could you move out of some of your busyness to make truer contact? How could you be giving yourself more? This allows you to feel the greatness of your generosity, to feel your best self, because the more you give, the more you know who you truly are. Sometimes when you feel you have nothing left to give, if you ask for heaven's help, you will find you have just what is needed, just enough to move you forward and get you back in the flow again.

Close your eyes, and imagine God pouring down all kinds of energy and light. As you are filled with this energy, feel how you are motivated to give, especially in certain areas. What are they? Maybe you are called to give very simple things. Even the simple things can show your love.

217 Fantasy is a way of not communicating your needs.

In fact, you are hiding what you need. You imagine what you think would nurture you, excite you and make you feel good, but all of this actually comes between you and your partner. Fantasies cannot really satisfy you, because rather than allow for change, they support the status quo, and only compensate for what is missing in your life. You fantasise to give yourself relief, while the real relief is in moving forward. You can only begin to change the situation by communicating about your needs and giving through them.

Check out the fantasies you have in your life. Do you make pipe dreams about what you are going to do later, or what you are going to do with your partner? Now is the time to let go of all those things you are going to do in the future, or all the things in your mind you are using to excite yourself. Really communicate with your partner. Really make contact because this is the way to move through your needs and into a sense of satisfaction and a new level of receiving.

218 The extent to which your heart has been broken is the extent to which you will break hearts around you.

When you have had your heart broken a number of times, or even just one good time, you move into independence so as not to be hurt any more. This dissociation is an unwillingness to be captured, or once again, thrown into sacrifice or love slavery. In this unwillingness to deal with your feelings, you take the independent role, and because of it you become very attractive.

Self sufficiency fosters a certain attractiveness, which moves people toward you, but it also has a way of bringing out their dependency. Of course, when their dependency comes out, they try to get you to meet their needs, and they try to capture you in relationship – all the things you vowed would never happen again. Naturally, you move away from these situations where you can be manipulated or where you have to deal with your own feelings – and then hearts begin breaking around you.

The extent to which your heart was broken is the extent to which you will not be responsive to the needs of the people around you. When you are willing to deal with your own heartbreak, your old hurts, and your own needs, you will find within yourself a greater willingness to be responsive, and to communicate with people around you so they do not hurt themselves. Communicate your truth, what it is you want – but in a responsive way that helps and supports others to move through their own painful experience.

Be responsive to someone around you who is in need because your responsiveness to them heals you both.

219 Under every power struggle is an old heartbreak.

We have power struggles to protect yourselves. In a power struggle, two people are polarised. The other person acts out behaviour that got you heartbroken before – maybe not exactly the literal behaviour, but something metaphoric or essential to the old situation. Your unwillingness to move toward the other person is really your unwillingness to move toward and through this old heartbreak. You are afraid the same thing will happen all over again, and you will be wounded once again.

Today, look at a place where you are in power struggle and be willing to uncover it, and share your side of it. What is going on for you? Be willing to talk about what broke your heart long ago because communication is the end of this power struggle and the beginning of healing.

Intimacy creates healing.

The closer you get to a person, the less any problem can stand between the two of you. Intimacy creates the safety for communication to occur and the closeness by which old pain can come to the surface. The very word "intimacy" comes from the Latin term, "in" and "tim re," which means "not to fear."

All of us have a basic primordial fear that, "If a person gets to know me, they won't like me." Often after the beginning stage of a relationship, people quickly drop their partner because of their fears that they are unlikable, that once people know them, they will lose all their attractiveness. But the willingness to maintain intimacy creates the courage to move past the initial fear.

Think of someone with whom you could create a greater sense of closeness – maybe your partner, or one of your parents, or a friend. Be willing to move toward them and create that atmosphere of safety and warmth and intimacy that will lead to healing.

221 Ask for Heaven's help if you reach a state of valuelessness or meaninglessness.

Sometimes, in the circumstances of life, we experience such deep loss or disappointment that we are knocked out of the game of life, or thrown into the ashes. We may have set our mind on some goals, and when we reached them, we realised that it was nothing like what we thought it would be. People can spend their whole life working on a project, and when they get to the end of it, they sometimes feel it was all useless. But valuelessness and meaninglessness are states of consciousness just this side of enlightenment. When you are in these states, all you need to do for a major breakthrough is ask for heaven's value or meaning for you.

Meaninglessness, which is one of the most painful experiences, is the battleground of the ego and your Higher Self. Your ego is trying to take you on another useless crusade, to get you to think meaning is to be found somewhere in this world. But when you ask for heaven's meaning, you will hear a quiet voice saying very simple things, like "give," or "love," or "be happy." These words carry with them the grace to move you forward and experience the grace of the directive. It is quite the same with valuelessness, which blocks mastery. It can also be easily transcended this way.

Whatever state you are in, clear your mind. Whenever a thought comes up, just say, "This thought reflects a goal that is keeping me from true meaning or value." After about ten minutes, when your mind is cleared, ask for heaven's value and meaning for you. The words that come in will bring true peace to you, and grace will bring true fulfilment with the words.

222 The grass is always greener over the graveyard.

This is a conspiracy the ego has for us which tries to trap or delay us. Here are two common traps of relationship: You are in a relationship with your partner that you have been in for a while. All of a sudden, someone comes along who seems much more attractive. Since the first stage of relationship is the romance stage, anybody new will be attractive. Now if you are in a power struggle with you partner, or working through the dead zone, anyone will look more attractive. Of course, if you went on with the new person, you would eventually reach power struggle and dead zone with them too.

Another common trap is when our mind begins thinking about someone we were with in the past. The key to the traps is that your happiness is some place other than where you are. The ego works to trap you out of present, possible happiness.

Appreciate the situation you are in now. Really appreciate your partner and everything about your life. You can enjoy the connections with integrity that you have with everyone around you, without losing your present happiness. Remember, it is common to have your ego dream about someone you used to be with to make the present relationship tasteless. In which case, you move on, and later end up fantasising about the relationship you just left, and the one from before that. Do not fall into the trap of thinking the grass is greener somewhere else.

223 All relationship triangles are a form of competition rooted in our original, unbalanced family.

The imbalance created a sense of scarcity where we felt we had to compete both for love, and to have our needs met – to grab our share before everyone else did. This unhealed family situation throws unhealed people out into the world. There, the old competition for Mum or Dad's love is replayed through triangle relationships, whose purpose is to keep us from moving forward. Although this is one of the best traps of the ego, almost all families can be better balanced and come to a greater state of bonding.

Imagine going back to your original family situation and supporting yourself as a child to be strong enough to support the rest of the family. Support brings balance and ends competition; healing the unbalance in your mind brings healing into your present situation.

If you are in a triangle relationship, being willing to move forward will allow the person who is true for you to move forward with you. Just ask for the next step beyond the triangle situation. Trust in yourself and in heaven that your true partner will come forward ready to commit to you, that it will be the one who has the best qualities of both people. And you will no longer have to fear losing something or someone in the triangle.

If we value ourselves, we find we are creative enough to reach a solution without having to give up our position or our selfhood. Sacrifice comes from the illusion that if we give up our own self, we can let the other person carry us forward. We willingly do anything for a person just so we can use their selfhood for our sense of identity. Of course, our sacrifice cheats our partner as well as ourselves: we cannot receive their gifts, and they get what we consider to be damaged goods – not our true selves.

Today, begin to value yourself and find your true centre. Live your truth rather than someone else's. Give yourself the most valuable gift of all – you. Ask your Higher Mind to carry you back to your centre. It is a place of peace, innocence, true value and relatedness.

225 What you give creates your experience.

Meaning and value in life come from how much you give. If you are giving very little, you will find that the situation has very little for you. If you are giving all of yourself, you will find that the situation brings you back to yourself multiplied.

Today is a day where you can increase the value of what you receive by totally giving yourself. What you give creates your experience. What you give to your partner allows higher meaning to emerge in your relationship. The more you give today, the more you will receive.

226 Fear comes from attack thoughts, grievances, or complaints in your own mind.

But many of us think fear comes from something outside us. Since the mind works in terms of projection, we naturally see the world responding to us as we are thinking. When we send out attack thoughts, we see the world as attacking us back, and as a threatening place. So we feel frightened. But the fear began earlier in our own mind.

The opposite of fear is love. And our love – the natural extending of ourselves to the situation and people around us – creates healing. Any blessing you give is one you get to receive, and it heals your attack thoughts and your fear.

Today, be willing to change your fear or attack thoughts into love thoughts, into blessings. Bless someone around you. Wish the very best for them. Give them a gift of your energy, which will then multiply both for them and you.

227 Every power struggle hides a birth.

Would you like to get over this long, drawn-out war, this power struggle? You can if you have the courage to experience what is under every power struggle – a place of feeling so painful you will do anything to avoid it. You would rather have a war on the outside and suffer this pain over a long time than experience it all in a few moments or a few hours. Yet, your willingness to go to this depth of feeling will take you to a place of new birth where you can choose to give to someone. Giving uses some of the most creative energies of your mind to bring about a whole new situation of love, transcendence, vision and purpose.

If you choose, you can take a giant step today. Your awareness of that place of birth and the willingness to find it allows it to show itself. As soon as you experience it, give. Your giving will transform the pain into a new area of transcendence.

228 Ease is holding nothing back.

Ease is a living partnership with your Higher Power, family, loved ones and all with whom you work. When you venture everything, giving one hundred percent, you receive from yourself and from life, and everything moves into ease.

If you are withholding yourself in any way, things will become difficult. Difficulties come from guilt and a certain belief that we can pay for our guilt by giving ourselves a hard time. It is as if we are saying, "I must be a good person. Look at how hard my life is." We compensate for our guilt with roles, rules and duties, which as defences do not allow us to receive. Instead, they lead to difficulties, being stuck, and feelings of deadness.

Rather than doing things out of rote and habit today, choose to give yourself fully in any situation, and ease will move life and opportunities toward you. Ease moves you forward in partnership. It always says, "We can do this together. We can move forward together in such a way that no one loses." You know this because you have given yourself fully. Together, nothing can stop you.

229 Sacrifice is counterfeit love.

While love extends itself and creates, sacrifice arrogantly abases itself. Sacrifice gives without receiving, and is therefore not a true giving. Sacrifice says, "I'm not okay. You are okay," thus cheating someone out of the greatest gift you can give – yourself. At the same time, it discredits any gift that is offered, for nothing is received. The feminine (the side of you that receives) remains unredeemed; there is no opening, no release.

Sacrifice is something we do to compensate for old feelings of unworthiness, guilt, and failure. It always tries to prove something it does not even believe itself. Sacrifice is based on giving up your identity to steal a more worthy self – the person for whom the sacrifice is being made.

Sacrifice is the most common form of counterfeit love, for it is a surreptitious holding back, and unwillingness to move forward and change. It is counterfeit commitment, which withholds the element most needed in relationships – your giving and receiving.

Today, it is time to move out of your sacrifice. Tell the truth to yourself. Know what it is you really want to do, and ask your Higher Mind to carry you to your centre. Recognise that what comes to you today comes out of your true giving.

230 Fantasy is a way of not unwrapping your presence.

It is a way of costuming everyone around you to fit your needs. Though we all have fantasies, it is important not to get caught there, because the more we are caught there, the less we show ourselves. Only after unwrapping and giving ourselves can we really receive the gifts of life. So while we may play a little bit in fantasy, we need to remember that it is who we really are that gives us satisfaction. Giving, revealing and opening ourselves with all of our desires, wants, needs, joys and satisfaction is what allows life to give to us.

Look at all of your fantasies – sexual fantasies, hero fantasies, fantasies about how life is going to get better. Be willing to let all these go. When you catch yourself in fantasy, just ask, "Who is it that really needs my help?" Then pour your love out to that person. As you do, you will feel a much greater sense of satisfaction and openness to receiving the gifts of life.

Do not put off enjoying these gifts to some time in the future. Do not wait for retirement to enjoy yourself. Do not wait until it is too late to begin to enjoy your partner: look at them, drink them in, feel them inside you, enjoy every gift they have. Do not wait to say how much you love and appreciate someone: appreciate the people who have really meant something to you in your life, contact them, and say thank you from your heart. Appreciation brings enjoyment. Do not wait to enjoy yourself, open yourself, and drink in life. Do not wait to take a full breath of the air of life, to take such a bite out of life that when the juices run down your face, everyone will lick their lips. It is all being given to you now. Open your eyes so you can see it.

231 **A relationship is not a fifty-fifty deal. It is a one hundred percent deal.**

If you are giving your fifty percent and waiting for your partner to give their share, you may be waiting a long time. In giving fifty percent, you may find that your partner is seemingly not giving anything at all. Yet the very things you complain they are not giving is what you have come to give in the relationship. In fact, any area that is not succeeding is an area in which you are not giving one hundred percent. If you give one hundred percent, the relationship will move forward and your partner will begin to give what they have come to give the relationship also.

Examine your life today, and see where you could make the simple choice to give a hundred percent and make your life and your relationship easier.

232 In your relationship you can choose drama or you can choose creativity.

We have drama so we do not feel bored, so we can feel alive and that something is going on with us. But if there is drama in your relationship, it means there is a misuse of your creative energy. But we could use all of this energy to find the solution rather than making the situation more dramatic.

Use your energy in a positive way. Look for creative solutions, and your creativity and contact with life will create all the excitement you need. It will allow you to feel your best self. Rather than creating more and more drama, or problems, or hysteria in your relationship, use your creativity to find the answers – express it as an act of love.

233 Creativity is the antidote to loss.

When we feel we have lost something, we tend to move into bad feelings, areas of fear, sadness and sometimes guilt. But we could use this situation as an opportunity to become creative, which would free us from the sense of loss. By taking all of the energy in this painful situation and transforming it for our own healing, it would be a gift of love to those around us, and an antidote to their loss also.

Look at any situation where you feel a sense of loss, or a fear of loss. This is the place to become creative. Just sit back, close your eyes, and allow to come into your mind how you might give out of your love and transform the situation through your creativity.

234 When you wish to have a need fulfilled, forgive.

Your forgiving takes away the judgement and the guilt. Removing the guilt allows you to move forward, and as you move forward, your need is fulfilled. Your forgiveness is also a giving forth; and every giving forth simultaneously gives to you and fulfils your needs.

List three major needs you have in your life right now. Ask yourself, "Who is it that I have not forgiven?" Do whatever it takes for you to forgive so these needs can be fulfilled, and you can come to peace. Sometimes when the situation seems beyond you, and the need seems impossible to fill, ask for your Higher Mind to come in and help complete the forgiveness. As the forgiveness is completed, you will come to peace and feel your own wholeness.

235 Without commitment to a common goal, any conflict could destroy a relationship.

But if you and your partner have a common goal or commitment that you have chosen together, then any conflict that comes up is just something to move through on the way to that goal. As you resolve each conflict, you build another layer of partnership.

Close your eyes and visualise your purpose in the relationship. What is it you want? What common goals have you chosen? Feel your partner arm-in-arm with you, moving forward in confidence toward this goal. Know that you can step through each conflict together on the way to the goal. As you commit, the power of the conflict is lessened and the power of the relationship is increased.

236 Heaven can only be entered now, never on an instant replay.

Many of us think back to idyllic times in the past – but those times are just something in our mind that we use to help make up for the lack we feel right now. Trying to live in the past does not make us happy. Replaying those idyllic times is really a lie, because, even during those times, there was something missing that we went on for. This time, this moment, is the chance we have to fully learn the lesson, and to gain a much greater sense of happiness.

Close your eyes and imagine that all the joy and happiness in the world was filling you up right now. Let it fill your body from your toes to the very crown of your head, everything within you. Feel it overflowing. This state of happiness, this heaven is within us now.

237 Your judgement throws you into sacrifice.

This is because when you judge you feel bad and unworthy, so you will act out a role to compensate for how you feel, to prove you are not like this. And because the role is solely concerned with proving that you are not bad and unworthy, it does not allow you to receive. Thus, you are thrown into sacrifice. Every judgement you can let go of, every person you can forgive saves you lots of time, and saves you from the unhappiness and unrewarding work of roles and sacrifice.

Imagine your mother as just a little girl, sitting on your lap and telling you about all the hopes and dreams that she had for you when she dreamed of having a baby. Then imagine your father as a little boy, sitting on your other knee, telling you of how he dreamed of growing up to be a man, having children of his own, taking care of them and giving his very best, so these children would feel loved. Now for a moment, remember how it was for you as a child – your desire to have things be better, to have children you would love, to give the very best to the people you love. Now, if you are willing, let go of your judgements on your parents. Given their upbringing, their background, and their inner and outer pressures, they did the very best they could. Every judgement you have on your parents locks you into sacrifice and roles. You can free yourself today by making a new decision not to be bound by the past.

238 If you do not have something in your life, it is because you are getting revenge.

All of us complain about what is missing in our lives. But take a deeper look at what you do not have, and what you want more of in your life. Then ask yourself, "By not having this thing, who is it I am getting revenge on?" It is always true to say "myself" – but that is not the whole answer. Revenge is always about getting back at someone beside yourself. So who is it you are getting back at? Is it worth it to keep up this power struggle that robs you of present happiness?

Now is the time to drop the revenge and let yourself receive.

239 **Sacrifice in the present comes out of a past judgement that our needs have not been met.**

This creates sacrifice for two different reasons: We either look for others to meet our past needs – which is impossible; or, because of our judgement, we take on a compensating role to show those people how it should have been done. On the surface it might seem as if we are doing things so much better than they did, but what is actually occurring is that we are in sacrifice and cannot receive. So we move into greater and greater burn-out. Once we understand and forgive the people in the past, we can move on.

Look at the areas where you are in sacrifice, and ask yourself, "Who am I still judging?" Ask that part of your Higher Mind in charge of forgiveness and illumination for the forgiveness to be accomplished, to free you from working so hard and receiving so little. Ask also that you be freed from those past hungers which cannot seem to be satisfied in the present.

240 Your happiness is the best gift you can give the world:

It is infectious, enlightening, and gives hope. It is a form of love that spreads around everyone. Imagine yourself as a parent, happy – how it would delight your children. Imagine yourself as a partner filled with the love that makes happiness – how that would touch your partner and overflow onto them. If a situation is stuck and you bring your happiness to it, the situation will move forward because there is so much creativity in happiness.

Many of us think our happiness depends on things outside us, and that we have to wait to be happy until some of these outside things are taken care of. Today, be that hidden agent. Be entirely happy, give happiness, for no good reason, for every good reason.

241 **If your partner loses, you will end up paying the bill because you are the other part of the team.**

So it is really important that you concentrate on moving through all forms of competition and power struggle into areas of support and cooperation so your partner always succeeds. Either you will get the benefit of every success they have, or you will end up paying the bill.

Today, no matter how you feel, give extra support to your partner to make sure they succeed. Their success is your success.

242 Love stops time and starts eternity.

In eternity there is a sense of pure creativity. Joy abounds and overflows. The extent to which there is love in our life is the extent to which we do not have to travel to go anywhere else. We do not have to work to get anywhere because love is here and now. Love says there is a never a means to an end. Love is always both the means and the end. If you could love powerfully enough, you could stop time. You could use the true sense of time, which is learning about love and healing ourselves. The place where time stops is a place where you could save yourself years and years of hard work and pain.

Allow that healing to come into your life now. Who could you be loving more? Who is right there before you? – your partner, to whom you could give so much love that time seems to stop and eternity begins.

243 Judgement is always of a person's body, personality, or mistakes.

If you look beyond that to the person's essence and gifts and to what is likable about them, to what you appreciate, your judgement will fall away. To see and join with this part of them is to free yourself, because judgement is always a two-edged sword that we use to attack others as we attack ourselves.

Close your eyes and imagine you are looking past the person's body, personality, and mistakes to what you appreciate about them. Then look beyond their gifts to the place inside them where their light shines. Sit before that light a moment. You cannot judge them when you look at the light of their spirit.

244 If you are working too hard in the present, you have not let go of the past.

Often we become so good at our work that when we work, we feel we are our best selves. But workaholism is a compensation for bad feelings, for something from the past, some judgement, conflict, or pain we are still hanging on to. As we let that go, we find we naturally move into a balance in our work situation – we work just enough and have the courage to deal with whatever feelings are coming up from within us. So if you want to find a way of working more truly and effectively, find what it is you are still hanging on to from the past, and let it go.

Today, examine situations where you seem to be working too hard, and life seems to be too much of a burden. Realise that is an area where you carry a grievance. Ask yourself what that is, and be willing to let it go today, because your grievance is killing you.

245 When someone gets angry at you, there is a lesson for you to learn.

So just listen. You have a certain responsibility for their anger. So do not say, “Oh, that’s just their problem.” At the same time, do not take on their anger and make it the end of the world. There is just a lesson for you to learn. Be aware, and you can use every opportunity, no matter how negative, to help you move forward. Let this anger awaken you to something about which you were asleep, that could help you progress.

Be willing to use any opportunity of anger as a time for self-examination. Do not fight against this anger, or run away from it, but listen to see what truly applies to you. The anger may be entirely misplaced, yet it can still serve to get you in touch with something that is vital to you.

Partnership is common purpose.

We have been partners with many different people. We were partners with each one of our original family members. We have partners in business, and our relationship is a partnership. In all partnerships, the extent to which we live in a common purpose is the extent to which we succeed. Moving together in common purpose creates ease and flow, and allows grace to be present. In partnership, achievements and opportunities naturally come your way.

Starting with your most important partnership – the one with your love partner – see your common goal, and see yourself moving together toward that. Then see all the other partnerships you are in with your children, your parents, your siblings, your business partner, your creative partners and anyone else. See your common goal, and once you see it, notice how it attracts you, how it calls you and how you move forward effortlessly.

247 **Mastery in a relationship is a willingness to be innocent with those you love.**

To achieve innocence is to achieve mastery because you do not have to go anywhere; life always happens in the here and now. Innocence says you no longer have to punish yourself, or prove yourself – which takes lots of time and does not really work because it is a compensation for a negative belief. But once you know your innocence, you are free from the vicious circle of pain and compensation. You then allow yourself to receive, and invite the world into your heart. Through your innocence, your partner becomes a source of healing, wonder and enjoyment. Innocence allows you to give the best gifts of life by your being. Innocence is fun and playful, but most of all, it is the very truth about you. When you are willing to live this truth, then you create a power that is a source of healing for the world and especially for your partner.

Close your eyes and imagine that you stand before God who knows you to be truly innocent. For that which is innocent knows only innocence, and that which is Love knows only Love. Only your arrogance would judge you otherwise. Today let go of anything that stands in the way of your innocence, because it is one of the greatest gifts you can give to the world. The more you recognise your innocence, the more you can give love, and the more you can see and receive all the love that is being given to you.

248 All holding on is fantasy.

When you are holding on, you are living in the past, which is just living in a fantasy you have made up. Let go of the ghosts of yesterday. Holding on can never make you happy. Fantasy is an illusion. Let it go and allow yourself to receive what life has for you now because life has something better than what you are letting go of. It is something that is true for you, something that would move you forward, something that would let you really make contact and be satisfied.

What or who are you still holding onto now from the past? If you are still holding onto a certain quality about someone, let it go. Otherwise, your mind will be satisfied with the image and will not create that experience in your life now.

249 All problems are the result of amnesia.

We are all amnesiacs in that we have forgotten we are all a child of God, which is the very thing that would fulfil us and make us happy. We are the spiritual prince and princess of a kingdom we left long ago who have forgotten that we have a rich Father. Happiness, healing and forgiveness are all about remembering who we truly are and what we have come here to do. As we join with other people and begin to see no separation, judgement, or fear between us, we remember ourselves and our oneness.

As you remember who you are and what you have come to do, you will find the peace that is full of empowerment, the peace that heals. You will know everything is coming your way, that all things work toward betterment, that God is always looking out for you, loving you and taking care of everything.

Close your eyes, and go to the deepest part of yourself. Remember who you are and what you have come to do. Remember the kingdom you left so long ago that still awaits you. Remember that you are the light, that the light is your ally. You serve the truth and you have come to touch the world. Remember the legacy and all the joy that belongs to you.

250 If you do not have something in your life, it is because your guilt blocks it.

Guilt is the great spoiler. It blocks our receiving because we feel we do not deserve to receive. Of course, our natural tendency when we do not have something in our life is to blame someone else, especially our partner. We believe they are not doing something they could be doing, which would somehow make it all better for us. But if you took a deeper look, you would see that guilt blocks you from receiving. When we feel guilty, we have a sense of unworthiness and feel we do not deserve all the good things of life. But guilt is a mistake.

Imagine for instance that you had a child who made a simple, little mistake, and that child spent the rest of their life blocking out your love, and all the gifts you and everyone else wanted to give them. What would you be feeling about this guilt? Wouldn't you want to intervene and help your child find their innocence? Most of our guilt comes from similar circumstances, from patterns generated from mistakes in childhood. When you know your innocence, you can help those you love to find theirs.

Today, talk to the child within you. Tell them of their innocence, and help them see they did the very best they could. Forgive your child so your child will set you (the adult) free, and allow you to receive the love and gifts you so richly deserve.

251 Please touch.

Touch confirms, validates and heals. When you are in the midst of a power struggle and you touch your partner, you reaffirm that there is something greater than the misunderstanding. The more you can touch your partner, the more connectedness you create. Your touch is so healing and reaffirming that it alone creates the intimacy needed to resolve the problem. Your touch gives hope.

Today, be willing to touch your partner, your children, your parents, your friends. Shake hands, hug, or just put your hand on someone's shoulder. Today, give the sense of confirmation that touch brings. Caress your partner. Give them the touch that reaffirms life and says, "You did a good job. Thank God you are my partner."

252 The guilt you accept from others is only the guilt you are already feeling.

People can accuse you of all kinds of things – of being a bank robber, a sexual pervert, being too selfish, or not being a good parent. But the only accusations that bother you are the ones about which you are already feeling guilty. Nobody can make you feel guilt that you are not already holding in some part of your mind.

Today, when someone triggers your guilt, use the opportunity for healing. Know that this is a place where you feel guilt and stopped yourself from growing. Now you have the opportunity of transforming your guilt. No one has power over you that you are not giving them. Nobody can make you feel bad except where you already feel bad. Say to yourself, "Now that I am in touch with this feeling, I can do something to change it. I know this guilt is an illusion and that it is based on a mistake. I will learn the lesson now and move forward in my life. I will feel it until it disappears. For today, I choose to receive."

253 What you fight against, you become.

In other words, we take on the qualities of whatever we are fighting against. At the same level, a rebel always harbours a tyrant within himself. In our personality, when the rebel knocks off the tyrant who has been running us, the rebel becomes the leader. But unfortunately, given time, the rebel within will manifest traits similar to those of the tyrant. Everything you resist, persists.

See what you are fighting against today, particularly the quality within that you seem to be fighting. Close your eyes and allow yourself to drift back to that place in your life where you believed you had the same quality before you hid it away. Naturally, in believing something about yourself so strongly that you hid it away, you will create someone in your life to act out the particular quality. But the more you fight against it, the more this particular quality will come to the fore in your life. So today, go back to that part of you that you hid away. Take it in your arms, reassure and accept that part of you. Understand what a difficult situation you were in then. As you foster that part of yourself, you will find that it will begin to grow until it reaches your present age. Then it will naturally melt into you, and you will find that this resistance or fight that has been outside yourself will just disappear.

254 Feeling your feelings is a basic form of healing, letting go, and moving forward.

If you feel your feelings until they transform, the negative becomes positive, and the positive increases. You know that the pain you are feeling is an illusion – a mistake, but you are willing to feel it because it is your experience. When the negative emotion is gone, you come to a whole new level. Every time you feel your feelings, you end your denial, let go of the past, and allow yourself to move forward – it re-associates you.

By the time we get to independence, we have dissociated thousands upon thousands of feelings. Dissociation is the counterpart to hysteria. Although hysteria seems to feel lots of feelings, it still avoids the true feeling. Our willingness to be aware and experience our true feelings leads us out of deadness and into partnership, where we can experience joy and receive.

Remember today that feeling your feelings is the key to enjoying life. So just allow yourself to feel more. You may notice a time lag between choosing to do this exercise and becoming aware of your true feelings. This merely speaks of the amount of dissociation that you are in now. Some people even take a week to really get in touch with what they feel. But whatever your time lag, be willing to start. To the extent you are truly re-associated with your feelings, you will allow success and its enjoyment into your life, through knowing yourself and embracing life fully.

255 **Deadness in a relationship can be healed by asking for Heaven's help and moving toward your partner.**

When we feel dead in our relationship or so stuck, weary, or disinterested that the resistance seems beyond our ability to get through, we can ask for Heaven's help. Doing this is asking for that part of your own mind, your Higher Self, to give you enough energy at least to take the next step. You may be in a place where you feel there is nothing left to give, a place of such chronic exhaustion that you have to ask for help each step of the way. But the key is moving toward your partner, because once you have finally reached your partner, you find both rest and energy.

Look at a situation in which you feel stuck or too weary to move. Ask Heaven to help you join with your partner, and to move forward.

256 You can experience guilt only by living in the past.

But living in the past does not work because it no longer exists. When you are feeling guilty and living in the past, you are spending time in your mind instead of making true contact with those around you.

Today, let go of the past and the guilt. Let the lesson come forward and let yourself move on. As the guilt falls away, you will make better, more satisfying contact with everyone around you. Without guilt you naturally become more attractive, and life seems to treat you better.

257 "Shoulds" always express a conflict.

This is the reason none of your "shoulds" work. One part of you wants to do what you feel you should do, but another is resisting. Because of the hidden demands and needs within the "shoulds", the closer you get to what you feel you should do, the greater the resistance.

There is no reward for the things you feel you should do because you feel you have not chosen it, that it is just something you have to do, you've got to do, must do. So today let go of all your "shoulds", and allow yourself to choose. Choosing and setting goals sets up a flow.

258 **Love wants to give everything, totally, while holding on to nothing.**

It has no expectation and no conditions. It is not a contract – "I'll give you this if you'll give me that." When you give everything and hold on to nothing, a great sense of power, love and creativity emerges in you. Your heart opens. Time is transcended. You seem to move into a higher state of consciousness, where everything becomes tinged with colour and full of love.

Remember today that love is giving everything while holding on to nothing. Anything you hold on to, any contingent deals or attachment, blocks your enjoyment and receiving. Holding on is just a way of trying to make yourself safe. Love does not make you safe, it makes you real, makes you alive, makes you remember God. It makes you remember how much love is everything you ever wanted.

259 Being true to ourselves means we cannot be false to anyone.

If we are true to ourselves and stand in our own centre, we have a natural direction and purpose to our lives. But sometimes people become uncomfortable when we move into our centre, because living our truth reawakens them. It asks them not to live comfortably in areas where they are stuck in roles and duties. But even though we make them uncomfortable, we cannot betray them. Being truly committed to yourself, you could not betray anyone. Your truth for you allows you to extend the truth to others and for them to take their next step also.

Take a look at all the different areas where you could be truer to yourself. Where you are true to yourself, you are not overworked and in sacrifice. You are receiving reward, and things naturally flow with a certain ease. Where something is difficult, you are not being true to yourself. While doing something for approval seems to help you in the short run, it will lead to failure in the long run. Now is the time to be true to yourself, and in living this truth, to be true to everyone else.

260 If you do not have something in your life, it is because you are in a power struggle.

If there is something you think you want in your life, but it is not there, ask yourself this question, "With whom am I in a power struggle? Who am I fighting?" (In this exercise, the answer "myself" or "everyone" is a form of avoidance).

Put what you want in your life down in one column. Then allow to come to your mind who you are fighting, and put that in a column alongside the first. It could be your parents, your partner, God, or someone who is now dead. Now ask yourself, "Would I rather have the power struggle, or the things that I really want?"

A power struggle is really a place where you are using someone to avoid the real issue, the fear underneath. It is just a way of holding yourself back because you are actually afraid of what you want. Now make a third column, and write down what the fear is that holds you back from what you want. Let go of the power struggle. It is not true anyhow.

261 Sexual deadness in your relationship can be healed by taking the next step.

When the sex in your relationship is dead, look where you are stuck. At some level, you are afraid of moving forward. But your willingness to do so will take you out of this place of weariness, moving forward, for at least a little while. Your taking a step forward may not be the answer for the rest of your life, but it will be the answer for tonight. And that is just enough for now.

Close your eyes, and imagine you are in that place of deadness in your relationship. Now imagine that you begin to sink through the ground. Now, just find yourself sinking through all the layers of ground, passing through that place where you are stuck, until you get to a space that seems really open, really free, a place where you can really breath. No matter how stuck you are with a little willingness, you could just make the choice to move forward.

262 Jealousy is a birthing place.

It is also one of the worst feelings we can have. When we are feeling it, especially strong jealousy, brain waves of tantrums are perking though our mind. But they are also the brain waves of our most creative states. So you can turn this tantrum into a place of birth by giving totally. As you give through your jealousy, the place where you were stuck becomes a leaping-off place into your future, into higher consciousness and love. As you leave your attachments and needs behind through this birth, you will find more about what unconditional love truly is, creating a whole new level of love for yourself. No one can stop your love.

Imagine a wall of jealousy between you and your partner – a wall of tantrum. Today give through your jealousy by pouring your love through this wall or by being in service. Service helps you extend yourself through the wall. In this way, the pain is transcended without the necessity of suffering, and a new birth is brought about in the easiest way.

263 Your success in living your purpose is determined by the extent to which you forgive and integrate your parents.

Living your purpose is not necessarily something that you do, it is something that you are. To the extent you forgive your parents and give to them, you give the gifts that free you and allow you to learn what your purpose is. To the extent you are willing to balance both parents so that you are in the same love and harmony with both of them, you allow yourself to integrate the psychological poles that they represent for you. Forgiving your parents and balancing your love for them allows you to know that you can have a balance in both relationships and work. As you integrate your parents, you will become more and more creative; you will find the treasure that each of them is for you, and naturally extend yourself to them. Remember, what you complained your parents did not give to you, is what you came to give to them.

Feel what it is you have wanted, but did not receive from your parents. Now, imagine yourself as a child giving those gifts to your parents. After you give these gifts to them, see yourself throwing your arms around each parent. Then imagine and feel both of you melting together into pure energy. From this energy emerges the new you.

Tonight, with your partner, let down all of the walls that stand between you and them. Invite them into your heart, fully into you. Let no disagreement or condition stop you. You have been sent by All That Is to invite them home, which is through your heart. As you bring them fully into you, you will find a pathway opening up that will take you all the way home. Here you can see yourself and the path to Heaven they are. Here you can even see the face of God. Now it is time to celebrate the gift your partner is in your life. Invite them into you tonight, and you both will become more.

264 Only a willingness to take the next step allows you to see what it is.

Many people run around asking what their next step is, feeling they have to see it before they are willing to take it. But in truth, if you knew what it was, there is a good chance you would not take it – even if you knew it was the best thing you could do. So, only when you have a total willingness is the next step shown to you. As you move forward, you will find that you reach a place that is much better than where you are now.

Become totally willing for the next step to come to you. It will move toward you because of your choice, your willingness. Allow no distraction or temptation or problem to get in your way. Say yes to life.

265 Whatever the conflict, you are only fighting yourself.

Everything that happens in your relationship reflects a part of your own mind. If you were to heal the inner fight, the conflict between your partner and you would also be healed.

Stop fighting yourself in the guise of your partner. Be willing to accept the part of you that your partner is showing you. As you bring acceptance into any conflict, you will find a new confidence about moving forward. There is something much greater for both of you.

Whoever you are in a fight with, imagine them as wearing a party mask. Unmask them, and imagine it is you inside. How old are you? Whatever your age, ask yourself, "How is it that I may help you?"

What is asked for, and what you give to that part of you is the very gift the person you are in conflict with needs also. As you give it to yourself, you naturally give it to the person you had been in conflict with. And both of you move forward.

266

If you are not in beauty, wonder and joy, you are in judgement.

We know that when we are having a bad time, we are in judgement. But any time we are not enjoying ourselves, or experiencing the beauty within and around us, or we have lost our sense of wonder, we are also in judgement of something or someone. Who is it? What is it that you are judging? It is robbing you of a really good, creative time. Make a new choice today. Do you want the judgement or the enjoyment?

Allow to come to your mind what or who you are judging. You may find a long parade of people coming toward you. Be willing at this point just to forgive them. Bless each person who comes to you today so that you may begin to experience the beauty, the wonder and the joy in life.

267 Heaven can only be entered two by two.

Heaven is a state of consciousness full of joy, love and ecstasy. This state of love which opens Heaven can only be entered through forgiveness, surrender, and creativity – all of which involve togetherness. Thus Heaven can only be entered two by two.

While every grievance holds you both back, your forgiveness frees the other and yourself. And whereas hell is a state of consciousness of feeling utterly alone and tortured, Heaven is a state of sharing and oneness.

Let come to your mind the person who can best lead you into Heaven. It may be someone you are having the hardest time with, or it may be the person you are loving the most. Feel yourself bridging the gap between that person and you, forgiving them, reaching out for them, accepting them, and pulling them into you. Feel the light within you joining. And as you do, feel that sense of joy within you grow.

By doing this, you take one of the highest forms of consciousness and allow it to begin the process of making joy and healing. Let's say something that appears dark is given to you. For you to bring celebration into it might seem like an act of courage at first. But for you to celebrate what seems to be dark allows for the dawning of the light and any solution in the situation to begin to show itself. Celebration in the darkness allows for every element that is in the highest place of love and joy in the human race to show itself.

Celebration allows the love in the situation to be shared among everyone, and it is through love that people can bear up under anything. Love allows them to transcend whatever physical, emotional or mental lesson there is for them to learn. Celebrate what is given to you, turning whatever is given to you into a gift. And if it is a gift you receive, celebration lets you experience it fully. Celebration is the true state of the universe.

Today is a day for dancing the great dance of life. Whatever is given to you, make the most of it, find the joy in it, celebrate. Do not be caught by the disguises and illusions of the world. Find that the heart of everything has to do with joy, love, and celebration.

269 We create drama and pain in order to feel alive if feeling is shut down.

We cannot feel the energy within us or the natural excitement of our emotions as they run through us, so we create drama or pain to make ourselves feel something. When people have not been able to feel, they often go to greater and greater lengths to feel something – sometimes even to the extent of creating violence. Our willingness to feel, to open ourselves up, brings us back to feeling alive without having to create drama, negativity or pain.

When you are fully aware of any emotion, you feel excitement, because you are aware that you are healing, aware of all the nuances of the sensations as you feel them. And what we call emotion and pain is really just how energy expresses itself in certain situations. So today, allow yourself to take the time simply to feel things, to experience and embrace every sensation. This will allow both physical and emotional pain to release and unfold. Pay attention to exactly how the energy manifests itself.

Take a situation that is dramatic, painful, or unpleasant, and allow yourself to concentrate and accept the strongest sensation. Then allow yourself to feel fully how it changes, or how the next strongest sensation comes up. If you apply yourself to this, you will find a self-healing method you can use in any situation. Healing through experiencing ourselves feels good. Moving forward feels good.

270 Any area that is not successful in your present relationship is a result of competition.

Competition is a lower form of consciousness that can lead to power struggle and deadness, and can wreck your relationship. In subtle, or not so subtle ways, competition stops partnership, blocks cooperation, and interrupts success. In competition, each person fights for themselves rather than working for the partnership to succeed. Each of you will be trying to take care of your own needs, rather than working together and finding common purpose. One partner or the other will believe that they are the superior or the inferior one. Neither belief will support the relationship.

Take a look at where you are not succeeding in your relationship. What are you competing about? When you have found some answers, share these with your partner. Apologise, and as you begin to acknowledge these things about yourself, you will find that the relationship leaps forward. Your openness and your willingness to heal all the hidden aspects in the relationship will allow for intimacy, contact, and communication.

271 A relationship is about stretching and extending, not the stretch marks.

Stretching is about growth and taking risks into whole new areas, extending yourself beyond your comfort zone. Your stretch marks, on the other hand, are all the scars of the past, the dark lessons that have not been learned yet. They are what you show to prove how hard life has been and therefore how virtuous you are: "Look how hard this period of my life was. Look at what it did to me. Aren't I tough? Aren't I good?!" Sometimes stretch marks are there to prove your own self-concepts or to pay off guilt, which demand lots of time and energy but are never successful.

A relationship is not about scars, past or present, but about the gifts you have found in yourself as a result of reaching beyond your own indulgence and the sacrifice of roles and duties to find the truth. As you truly give yourself within a relationship, you learn how to relate without sacrificing yourself.

Look at your relationships, at what you have learned in each one and how much you have grown. Spend the most time on your present relationship, remembering who you were before the relationship began, and what was missing in your life. Remember what was present that you did not like.

Look at how both you and your partner have grown. Look at how much more mature, understanding, and patient you are. Look at how many hidden feelings have come to the surface to be healed. Look at the courage it has taken to deal with some of the conflict areas within your own mind, how you have dealt with the feelings about yourself that you had hidden away under roles, under things that just looked good.

272 As you do, you will find that a natural gratitude comes to you, for yourself, your partner, and the relationship.

273 You can be in Heaven with every person you meet.

Could you allow yourself to feel that wonderful with every person you meet? You could. You could make the choice to give someone your judgements, or your love. The decision you make shows what you think of yourself. To be in Heaven is just to give everyone you meet that much of you. This knocks the hell out of the other person and allows them to be in Heaven with you.

Be in Heaven with everyone you meet. Give them that much. Have that good a time. Dance! Your Higher Mind is dancing, so allow yourself to dance with joy with every person you meet today, tomorrow, from now on. When you wake up, begin the dance.

274 **The greatest art is the art of being yourself.**

This naturally proceeds from living your purpose rather than living for approval. Your purpose is what you – of all the people in the world – can do the best. If you do not do it, if you are not true to yourself, who will be? Who can be? It is left undone until you are willing to give your part and be yourself.

Your purpose leads to your fulfilment. Yet, most people are frightened of their purpose and the greatness that it seems to call from them. But in being frightened of your purpose, you are frightened of your own love, passion, and happiness. Most people feel unworthy, or try to control the good feelings so as not to be overwhelmed. These are just symptoms of fear that lead you away from your truth, your vision and your greatness.

Imagine that you are painting a beautiful masterpiece. This masterpiece is you, the picture of your life. Being you is being the artist with an inspired hand, the paintbrush with true colours and the painting all at once. Being yourself in all of your grandeur shows how much you love the world; it is your gift to life.

275 You cannot meet past needs in the present.

Many of us choose partners to make up for the needs that were not met in the past. The problem with this is that we may begin to hold our partner hostage for what our past did to us. We try to control them and make them give to us in certain ways, to take care of us, to meet the needs of the past in the present situation – which cannot be done. Trying to live the past in the present limits your relationship, and limits your partner from giving you all they wish to give you. So be willing to let go of the past and really enjoy your partner as they are.

When you let the past go, healing occurs. And paradoxically, as you let the past go, you get to receive now what you were trying to get then. But if you try to remake the past, you always stay unfulfilled.

Look at situations that are unsuccessful, and imagine these as places where you are trying to get old needs met. Who did not take care of these needs? As you see the past begin to come up, be willing to let it go. Be willing to put it in the hands of God so you can go forward and enjoy everything that wants to be given to you now. Stop complaining about the flower that died. You are walking in the garden. Just raise your perspective and see how much beauty and fragrance is all around you.

276 Guilt reinforces what you are trying to escape.

When you have guilt, the thing you are trying to get away from is always on your mind at some level. And the simplest fact of psychology is that what you reinforce you make happen.

Because of this obsession, you may totally withdraw from yourself and from life so as not to make that mistake again. Or sometimes you do exactly what you do not like because it obsesses you. For example, if a person murdered someone, the guilt from that would either have them begin to kill themselves on the inside; or, they would once again have a certain violent desire to kill someone again – to defend against the guilt, creating a vicious circle.

Today, forgive yourself. Put your guilt in the hands of God. God knows better and only sees your perfection, and therefore knows there is nothing to be forgiven. We have all made mistakes, but mistakes can be corrected and the lesson learned. Guilt only holds us back from God and everyone we love. It is a self-destructive form of avoiding lessons, gifts and others.

Today, do not let your guilt come between you and anyone that you love. Do not let your guilt stop you from life. Today let your guilt go. Learn the lesson. Move forward. Your innocence heals the world.

277 Every swamp gets its rock.

This speaks of two completely different styles of communication in any given relationship. The swamp-like person is emotional, and tends to personalise communication. Whereas, the rock-like person tends to generalise, dissociate, and be abstract. Rocks tend to be stoic where swamps tend to be hysteric. Rocks deny themselves and go into sacrifice, where swamps are selfish and tend to indulge themselves. Swamps are natural talkers, and rocks natural listeners. Rocks always find themselves falling in love with swamps because they love the fluidity and the freedom in sexuality the swamp seems to exude. Whereas, rocks have lots of rules and sometimes purify the pond to the point where the water lilies die. Swamps of course always feel attracted to the confidence of the rock, to the one in control – at least for the first few minutes. After that, competition sets in. Rocks are natural givers, and swamps are natural receivers. Swamps can be supersensitive, where rocks seem to be impervious.

It is important to understand these styles of communication, because they form areas of power struggle and competition that carry over into the dead zone. With the realisation that each person is playing a role, the swamp can begin to firm up, and the rock to loosen up. When the competition is let go of, and the swamp moves its emotions into its natural waterways, springs gush forth out of the rock. This creates fertile land where the water flows.

Take a look at who is the swamp and who is the rock in your relationship. Begin to create a bridge toward your partner, because as you move forward together, both of you naturally win.

You will lose your partner's communication if you make it all about yourself.

This is important. Making every communication be about yourself, rather than about both of you, can destroy a relationship. Your relationship is not here just for you; it is there for both of you.

Now here is a problem that rocks and swamps get into in relationship: Swamps are natural communicators. They typically personalise things so they speak about themselves and their own feelings. Rocks are out of touch with their feelings. They tend to be stoic, and dissociate themselves. A rock will share their personal feelings about three major times in a relationship and typically only a total of seven times before giving up. On these rare occasions, they may open up their heart and talk about what they are experiencing.

Sometimes at this point, a swamp will indulge themselves and turn that personal sharing into an attack on themselves – which is just a way of stealing centre stage again. If the swamp takes the communication and uses it to bring the story line back to themselves, they have lost a major opportunity. It is important for swamps to recognise those rare times when a rock will take a risk and let down the drawbridge to show their deep, inner feelings. If the swamp succeeds in listening and supporting the rock's communication, the rock will take other risks.

If you are a rock, risk sharing what is really going on for you, and support your swamp by letting them know that your communication is not intended to make them feel wrong. If you are a swamp, go out to support your rock so that the rock will feel safe enough to lower the drawbridge. Sometimes when swamps encourage their rocks to share, and

278 they respond, the swamp runs. So be sure that when you are asking for the rock to share, you are not also pushing them away because you are afraid of what they might say. Do not let what the rock shares just be one more excuse to prove that you are unlovable. The rocks are just saying what they are feeling, and they need to get that out before they can move on. All they need is a little support and compassion. This is the time to borrow the rock's natural inclination and ability to abstract and to impersonalise what your rock is saying.

279 **Hysteria and stoicism are simply different forms of communication designed to avoid rejection.**

A swamp is naturally hysteric as a rock is naturally stoic. When rocks have unpleasant feelings, they try to suppress them and not let it bother them. They bury the feelings inside just to get through it. Swamps tend to cry about everything except the real feeling that is bothering them. In either case, both the swamp or the rock is seeking approval. But it only leads to power struggle and misunderstanding.

If you are the swamp, take a look at how you are avoiding what you are really feeling, what the risk would be. If you are the rock, get more in touch with yourself, and find what sharing you are avoiding. If you took the risk to share what are your major issues, you would make the relationship better.

Swamps feel unloved and rocks feel misunderstood.

No matter how much love swamps receive, they feel it is never enough. A rock feels that no one cares enough about them to really understand what they are feeling. Rocks are really clams because they have swamps inside them. But both sides are feeling a lack of support and understanding. A rock feels that a swamp just cannot support them, whereas a swamp feels they are just water off a rock's back. Swamps feel all the things that they were missing in childhood, so they make everything about themselves. Rocks feel there was not enough love to go around in their childhood, so they had to give themselves up, to sacrifice themselves.

In any kind of misunderstanding, rocks want to get to the bottom line and solve the problem. Swamps have no bottom line. They just want to be touched, felt, loved, understood and appreciated. In problem solving, swamps want to be touched first, and everything will turn out fine; rocks typically do not want to be touched until the problem is solved. Rocks tend to be visual – they see the world first. Swamps tend to be kinaesthetic – they feel the world first. Rocks cannot see what swamps are feeling, and swamps cannot feel what rocks are seeing.

Rocks tend to be heroes, even tragic heroes or martyrs. At some level they are trying to save others or the world because they believe deep down that they are lost. Swamps are just trying to save themselves, so they resent the time that rocks spend on others and not on them. In this way a swamp is correct: if a rock were truly to give them their time and energy, the joining that occurred would create the perfect balance and foundation for much greater success.

280 Talk to your rock or swamp about these concepts. Share the places where you are different, and communicate with each other about how you might find a common goal, and through that a greater understanding.

Rocks have amnesia and swamps never forget.

Rocks have amnesia because they tend to be thinking about what they consider to be bigger things. To a swamp, nothing is bigger than thinking about themselves. Rocks tend to forget important things like anniversaries and birthdays. They also tend to forget what happened in the past. But swamps never forget a date, an anniversary – and they will certainly never forget something that happened in the past that the rock has not apologised for yet.

Swamps need to share their feelings about the past. Rocks need to let swamps know that in spite of what was said or done, they really do love the swamp. Swamps have to be told time and time again that they are loved because they have all of this history in their minds to prove they are not loved. So they constantly ask to be reassured by the rock. Rocks have long since forgotten all about what they said or did not say, and feel telling their swamps that they loved them once should be enough. The rock's willingness to reach out to the swamp to reassure them, and the swamp's willingness to let go of the past allows for both of them to move forward together.

Rocks are natural givers, and swamps are natural receivers. Because rocks are natural romantics, if they remember to keep the romance in the relationship and to keep giving to their swamp in thousands of creative ways, they will constantly move the relationship forward. Swamps have a natural ability to receive what the rocks give them. But if swamps really want to move the relationship forward they can give to the rock.

Today, rocks remember your swamps. Move toward them to give to them. Remember all the important things and

281 relate to your swamp in a very personal way. Swamps, think about your partner for a change. Both of you, commit to your partner – in spite of their being a rock or a swamp. Really choose them because this commitment will bring you to the next stage, to a higher level of understanding and mutuality.

Being a rock means never having to say you are sorry.

Rocks hate apologising because it feels as if they are admitting to how incredibly guilty they feel inside. And they hate guilt because they feel that somewhere in their lives they have totally blown it, and have not really forgiven themselves for this. That is why they are trying to save the world. They feel as if they have made such a big mistake they need to sacrifice themselves. But whatever sacrifice they make can never make up for their guilt.

Swamps are always apologising and abasing themselves, not because they have done something wrong – but, because they feel they are wrong. "Being wrong" is why they believe they did not receive all of the love and attention they felt they needed as a child, and why the love they receive now is never enough. So no matter how much the rock sacrifices or gives to them, it is never quite enough to reassure them.

Swamps are also really good at communicating what is not working – at complaining or criticising. But rocks hate criticism, and will tend to overwork or learn things overmuch just so they will not be criticised. Rocks are always trying to prove how they survived in spite of how tough it was, sometimes doing stupid thing in testing their limits, always trying to prove themselves to get over the basic guilt. Their motto is, "No matter how hard it is, I can take it." But swamps can't take anything. If they get complaints or criticism, they tend to fold, disappear, run away or go into even more swamp-like behaviour. It is a perfect situation for mutual misunderstanding.

Spend time appreciating your partner. Each of you, in finding your natural partner, are acting out what the other is

282 missing. Together you can really balance and move forward. You can bring humour into the situation as you understand each other and the role that each of you has played. Now it is time to move out of these roles, and find a communication style that works much better for both of you.

283 You cannot get blood from a rock.

When rocks and swamps polarise, and go into a power struggle, it is not a pretty sight. Swamps get more swampy and needy, while rocks get even more rocklike, stonewalling their partner. They pretend nothing matters, and hold all of their feelings inside them, except when threatening to explode like a volcano.

The swamp will become a vampire, turning every little thing into an issue about themselves. They will try to suck any emotion, attention, love or any kind of energy at all out of the rock. The rock counters by becoming even more rocklike, developing a "you can't get blood from a rock" attitude toward the vampire. Typically, rocks were sucked dry as children by one of their parents so now they have a natural defence against vampires, and tend to withdraw, hide and disappear.

Imagine yourself as a child, and forgive the parent who was rocklike and did not seem to care for your needs, or the parent who was a vampire and tried to suck you dry. As a rock, you can ask for Heaven's help, and have all the energy of Heaven pour through you to fill your partner. As the swamp, you can ask for Heaven's help in truly giving to your partner. The acid test of true giving is to notice if the rock moves away from you or closes down. If they do move away, somehow you have been giving to take. Just ask for Heaven's help so that you can find within you the energy necessary to truly give to your partner.

Swamps want what rocks get but cannot receive.

When swamps and rocks are in polarised situations, rocks give to everybody else what swamps need the most. And because of rocks' natural generosity, they, in turn, receive a certain acclaim or acknowledgement from the world around them. But the acclaim rolls off their back, because rocks do not want to put their faith in something that might change. As children, rocks were happy. Then all of a sudden something happened, and their whole world came crashing down. So rocks do not tend to trust all the nice things that are said to them.

Swamps, of course would love to receive this kind of acknowledgment and recognition. They are sensitive and have natural compassion, but because they fear being overwhelmed with everyone else's feelings, they are afraid to move toward others. This is because, they not only feel their own feelings (which are almost too much), but they can also feel and resonate with what everybody else is feeling. It is as if they do not have natural boundaries.

While swamps are supersensitive, rocks have become impervious because at some early date they felt intruded upon, and emotionally raped. They are impervious to both the joy of giving and to someone trying to take, to receiving compliments and to receiving criticism. Swamps on the other hand are supersensitive. They revel in a good compliment, and a little appreciation goes a long way with them. At the same time, swamps have no ability to distance themselves from criticism, so it hits them hard. They cannot differentiate between the criticiser's projections, and what would be helpful for them to acknowledge. So, there is a tendency to attack back or abase themselves. It can get so overwhelming that they will limit themselves in their giving to other people.

284 Give what you want for yourself. If you are a swamp and you want recognition, give it. This will help you feel satisfied. If you are a rock, do not distrust what is being given to you as a means to trap you, but be willing to let it come deep inside you. You can be aware when people move from a mode of giving, to that of give-to-take. At that moment, you can communicate your own natural boundaries.

285 Rocks hate happiness because they are afraid of what might happen next.

They do not trust a good time, or a compliment. Rocks are unwilling to give up control to enjoy something, even for a short time; rocks know that when happiness occurs, a conflict is sure to follow. They never want to let themselves get soft, so they are always in a state of readiness for war. But they are good to have around in bad times because when the shit hits the fan, it is no surprise to a rock.

Whether you are a swamp or a rock, realise that after you have reached a new level of intimacy in your relationship, or a new height in your life, typically, you move from the mountaintop down into the next valley. Yes, the next conflict does occur, but only because you have reached a level at which you can now handle the next problem with true understanding and move through it easily.

Remember that answers come in at the same time as the problem, and that you do not have to linger in a conflict. The best way to move through conflicts is to be willing to give at such a level that you step from mountaintop to mountaintop.

If you are a rock and your partner is a swamp, you will think of the relationship as a rock does. You will experience it as somehow not nurturing you, and not giving you the understanding you need. The relationship will seem controlling and hard, and you will experience it as a sacrifice and a burden.

If you are a swamp and your partner is the rock, you will find the relationship swampy. It will not give you the support that you need, and it will not be personal enough for you. The relationship will take energy from you, energy that you feel should naturally be yours. At times, you will feel as if you have to walk on eggshells. The relationship will have lots of unfocused emotion and there will seem to be no clear direction for you.

Begin looking at your relationship from a larger perspective. Instead of looking at it through rock or swamp eyes, imagine that you and your partner were somehow melted down to your pure energy. Let all of this energy come together, and as it does, observe what is born out of it. You will find a whole new form for the relationship. You may feel the difference, or you may see the difference, but either way, it is a giant move forward.

287 What you hold against anyone keeps you from feeling loved.

When you have a judgement or grievance against anyone, you distance yourself and close the door to receiving. So what you hold against them blocks the way for you to feel love. The people around you may love you a great deal, but you are unable to feel that because you have closed the door and pulled away.

Let go of any grievances that you have toward anyone, and bless them. And as you bless them, feel yourself opening the door to receive once again all of the love and all of the abundance that is coming toward you.

288 **Vision is leaping the abyss to love, and leaving a bridge for others to follow.**

Vision means giving yourself so much that you turn yourself inside out. This kind of love, this kind of giving, leads you to see far into the future in a way that will work for everyone. It allows you to leap the abyss of the unconscious mind and to transcend nothingness. It allows you to move into a much greater area of love where you will see new answers. And as you see these answers, you are able to make a bridge for others to follow. You are able to find language to speak the unspeakable. When you are in vision, you are living your purpose. You are giving the gift of yourself in such a truly creative way that the path is made safe for those who follow behind you.

Know that what is before you is an opportunity for vision. Whether the situation is difficult or easy, love can be born at a much higher level. Your willingness to totally and thoroughly give yourself is the willingness to let this kind of love be born again on the earth.

When you feel you did not live up to your parents' expectations, it was actually that they did not live up to yours.

Many people believe they did not live up to their parents' expectations, and so they always feel inadequate. Some of these people move into perfectionism; others move further into that feeling of inadequacy, or even neurosis where nothing is ever good enough for them. If you believe you did not live up to your parents' expectations, it was really your parents who did not live up to yours. As parents, they were not good enough for you. No matter how your parents acted, this attitude is what keeps you feeling as if you did not live up to their expectations.

This is a three-part exercise. For part one, close your eyes. Imagine how your parents were when you were a child, and how you believed they were total failures as parents. Notice how you feel as a result of that attitude.

In part two, imagine your parents at the time. Pity them, feel sorry for them. They did not quite make it, but now you feel both above them and sad for them. Look at what you are feeling now in the situation, and how you feel about yourself.

And now the third part, imagine that your parents are still the way they were when you were a kid. See them as doing the very best they could, given what happened to them. When you look at them in these inner and outer circumstances, notice how you feel about them, and yourself. If you have done this experiment truly, you will begin to see that it is only your attitude toward your parents that dictates your experience of them. If your attitude did not produce the highest results, you can choose once again.

289 As another part of exercise three, imagine that you chose your parents for a specific purpose – that they reflect the most important yet projected areas of your mind that you came to heal, bridge and integrate. You chose them as the best people to learn what you have come to learn. Now, how do you feel? How do you feel about yourself?

290 **All accusations are self-accusations.**

Take a look at your world. Where do you feel grievances or judgements? Every place you accuse or attack other people is a place where you are attacking, accusing, or punishing yourself. It is a place where you feel guilty.

Today, learn true freedom. As you let go of your accusations against other people and become willing to give to them, remember that those people are only acting the way they are because they need something. If you are willing to give to them, support and forgive them, you will find that they blossom forth. To release yourself from the situation you feel stuck in, let go of your accusations and forgive the other person, because this will allow you to experience the freedom and innocence in yourself.

291 Your relationship will change as you change.

Here is the answer for creating quick change for yourself and your relationship: Stop complaining, stop blaming your partner, and give up your grievances. Your willingness to change yourself is what will make the relationship better. As you step forward, the attractiveness of that step forward naturally brings your partner along with you, and they begin to change. Wherever your partner is stuck, is an area where you are unwilling to step forward and change. Wherever your relationship is stuck, can be changed by your willingness to step forward. Your willingness naturally and easily moves you forward.

Look at what seems to be stuck in your partner and your relationship. How would you like to have it? Be willing to ask your Higher Mind to make those changes for you, to move you forward to where those changes could be made, so that your relationship, your partner and yourself will feel like the new improved model.

292 Your willingness to find what feeling the conflict hides creates a major growth opportunity.

Every conflict means there are hidden feelings on both sides. If you are willing to feel what you have hidden away, feelings you have not wanted to feel, and to burn through them, you will naturally move forward. The conflict situation will move up to a whole new level of healing and connectedness, where communication can begin.

If you are in conflict now, what is the feeling inside that you have hidden? Do not be afraid of it. Feel it. Burn through it until it is gone. As you do, everything will change for the better.

293 If you really want it, there is a way.

What makes this true is the power of the mind, and of choice. Your desire and your willingness always open the door for the solution to come in.

But you believe, you are in a situation where what you would get would hurt you – you are caught in a conflict. At that level, you always feel some ambivalence, and so you are not fully wanting it. But if you really want it, the miracle will occur, if necessary, for you to succeed.

Some people who are at the point of death ask for healing and it occurs, and they rise up to a higher level of understanding and life. Other people at the point of death ask for a miracle but are really afraid to receive one because a miracle would be counter to their belief system. They would rather die and be right than have to change their beliefs.

So if you are willing to change your beliefs and to change anything that is locked away inside you, there is a way, even if you do not have the vision to see it at this point. All it takes is for you to want it wholly.

Some situation in your life could come to a total success. All it would take is a few seconds of your focusing on that thing and totally wanting a way through. At that point, everything would begin to work out for you.

294 The greatest fear is the fear of happiness.

It is easy to see that people are less afraid of death than they are of happiness, because there are many more people who are dead or dying than happy. And even more rare are happy relationships. This fear of happiness can also be said to be the fear of Love, or the fear of God. To find God means that you would be totally obedient, you would have all the answers to your life, and you would be totally happy.

Your fear, then, is the fear of having to surrender this much, of having to let go of your way of doing things, of having to melt down all of the blocks, the controls and the rules that you have set up to live your life the way you do.

Today, let go of your thoughts about what brings you happiness. It is time to resign as your own teacher and ask Heaven to show you specifically what would make you happy, and to give you the strength to enjoy it.

295 We are always in the perfect place to learn the lesson we most need to learn.

If you have been following this book well, you will have begun to notice that everything seems to be connected, and nothing really happens by accident. We are always in the place that is perfect for us to learn what we most need to: "When the student is ready, the teacher appears." When you are ready, the situation is there to show you exactly what you are to learn and grow with at this point in your life; the people are there to help you move forward, to teach you, and to support you.

Take time to realise that you are in a perfect place for the lessons that you are learning, for the healing that you are doing, and for the growth that you are ready to make at this point in your life.

296 Your relationship to happiness is really your relationship to yourself.

It is what you are willing to give to yourself and to allow for yourself. So, how have you been treating yourself? We often do not recognise how much we are loved, and that we are given everything we are willing to receive. So, many blessings, gifts, happy experiences and joyful, loving situations pass us by just because we are not open to them. Your choice to allow more happiness into your relationship to yourself actually increases the happiness in every relationship you have, especially with your love partner.

Take a good look at how much happiness you are experiencing. No matter how much it is, you could be experiencing so much more. The key to increasing your happiness is in your relationship to yourself. Do not be so hard on yourself. Be willing to relax, and enjoy yourself today. Be willing to give to yourself today.

297 What you receive is what you think you deserve.

You could measure what you think of yourself and what you think you deserve just from what you are receiving. If you feel you do not deserve anything, you will not let yourself receive. You deserve it all – but how much are you letting yourself have?

Today is a day to acknowledge that you are worthy and that you have value because of who you are intrinsically, not because of what you do. You have value because you are a child of God who is loved and forever remembered in the Mind of God. You have intrinsic value because you have the ability to create and give life, because you, with your love, can bring the world to a new birth.

298 Your purpose brings fulfilment.

Living your purpose is one of the keys to finding happiness. Many people wonder what their purpose is – but your purpose is not really something you do, it is something you are. The more you unfold yourself, the more you develop yourself, the more you hear the call to what you truly want to do, the more you find your happiness. Doing what you truly want to do with integrity brings you happiness and fulfilment.

Be willing to listen to what it is you really want to do, and to follow that. It is the path leading home. Your purpose brings fulfilment, and your fulfilment is an incredible gift that you can share in your relationship.

299 **Those around you are in service to your mind. God comes at you in a thousand disguises to show you the ways that you keep yourself from God.**

Everyone around you is in service to you; they want to help you remember yourself. Each one of them is God calling to you. Be willing to move through all of the disguises and recognise God in everyone. Do not allow yourself to be stopped by your judgements, which, actually, are how you limit the people around you. They are also the hidden, or not so hidden, beliefs about yourself. If you do not love the people you can see, how can you love God who you cannot see?

Be willing to see God in everyone around you, and the situation will explode forward in joy and success, allowing you to feel the joy that is present at every single moment, and to feel how much you are loved.

With anyone who is close to you today, practice looking into their eyes, looking beyond their bodies, and see God smiling at you. See yourself recognising God in everyone, and enjoy the love and all the gifts God has for you.

300 Your relationship is the reflection of your belief system.

If you do not believe you can have it all in your relationship, you will get to be right. If you believe something about the opposite sex, you will get to be right. Anything you believe is what your relationship, your partner, and you will act out through your relationship. So if you do not like what you have, then change it by changing your mind.

Look at what your relationship shows. What does it show about men? about women? about sex? about love? about support? about communication? If it would be helpful, use a pen and paper to write down the above categories, and beside them write what is happening in your relationship. Next to that, write what your belief must be to have such a situation. Examine each of your beliefs, and whatever ones you do not like, take a moment for each and say, "This was a mistake. What I now choose is this ...". Thus you will use the power of your mind to move yourself forward.

301 All guilt creates withdrawal or aggression.

If you are feeling guilty, you will withdraw because you are afraid of doing the same thing over again. You will remove yourself from the path of life, or you will attack those around you to get away from the feeling. In the same way, if you lay guilt on those around you, you will find them responding either by withdrawing from you, or by becoming aggressive back to you. Everyone hates guilt. Guilt is the hot potato we always try to pass on to the people around us. We never want to take the responsibility for our guilt because it just feels bad. It is the destructive illusion that creates what it is trying to stop, either within or outside you.

Look at areas in your life that seem to express either withdrawal or aggression. These will be areas that are not working. Ask yourself what you must be feeling bad about to act in such a way. Your willingness to let go of your guilt, remember your innocence, support the people around you and yourself, allows you to move to a new level of success.

302 Your innocence is one of the best gifts you can give to your partner.

It is the extent to which you can freely love your partner and everyone around you, and the extent to which you can freely give the gift of your creativity to the world.

Your innocence blesses your partner and allows them to feel loved and cherished, and to feel what a treasure life is. Innocence allows your partner to unfold before you, and to give you all of the gifts and love they have ever wanted to. With innocence, you will feel totally loved, creative, and that everything is working out for you in every area of your life. (This would naturally make your partner's life a lot easier too.) Your innocence brings back enchantment, wonder, and a state of beauty to the relationship.

Innocence is a choice that we make. Today, choose to feel as innocent as possible in every situation. See any bad feeling as coming up just so you can let go of it. Welcome what comes up from your mind, or what seems to come from outside you, and let your innocence be the truth that accelerates all the bad feeling out of you. This way, you can receive all the gifts that are being given you, and give them back to your partner. Innocence is a state of being without guilt – which comes from within us, and from taking on jobs that do not belong to us, but to God. Innocence is knowing your true worth, knowing that you are valuable – not for what you are or what you do – but for who you are.

303 Your worry is a form of fear, and your fear comes from attack thoughts.

Your worry says that negative things could happen. When you worry about someone, you have no confidence in them or the situation. So you use the power of your mind to create a lack of confidence for them and to allow fearful elements in the situation.

Every time you feel tempted to worry about someone or something, give your blessing. Your blessing is your trust and your positive choice of the best thing to happen for everyone in the situation. Blessings are an antidote to worry. Your worry attacks the situation; your blessings build it.

304 What you love, you become.

We naturally gravitate toward what we love. And the more we do, the more we begin to enjoy ourselves, and begin to resonate with what we love. In this resonance, we find that what we love is within us also. This allows a giving and receiving in the love that lets us know it as ourselves. What you love, you plant in your heart and help grow like a beautiful flower. You want to give it to everyone else, so they can receive and enjoy what you are receiving and enjoying. Enjoyment always wants to be shared.

Look at who you love, and what you are really enjoying in your love for them. Allow yourself to feel your natural gratitude toward this person or situation. This allows you even stronger resonance with the gift you are experiencing. Your gratitude not only opens the door to love, it increases love.

305 Not trusting others is really not trusting yourself with those others.

You do not trust yourself not to be used, or taken advantage of in the situation, because you do not have confidence in this area. If you trusted yourself, you could be with the most seemingly untrustworthy of characters, and yet have the natural confidence to be with them and to create a successful situation. If you do not have that confidence, you could be with very trustworthy people, and you would feel betrayed because you lack the confidence to communicate what was vital to move the situation forward.

Look to see where you are not trusting people, and give confidence to yourself in this area. Trust yourself enough to communicate what you need to make the situation a greater success.

306 The extent of scarcity in a relationship is the extent of competition.

Any area in your relationship that is not fully abundant – communication, money, sex, free time, happiness, or whatever else – is an area where you feel that you are right, where you feel that you are a little bit better than your partner. It is an area in which you are fighting to get certain needs met from the situation before they do, or from them. The extent of scarcity is the extent to which you are not yet in partnership. All of us have many subconscious areas like this. Today make these areas conscious and make a new choice.

Look at the areas in which you would like to have more in your relationship, and begin building partnership in these areas. Begin supporting your partner because where you support your partner, the scarcity begins to fall away.

307 Never quit dating.

If you want to keep life in your relationship, keep giving life to it. Keep creating time for your partner and you to focus on the relationship itself, just enjoying yourselves and having a good time together. If you think you have gotten to know your partner, you are just deluding yourself unless you know their true greatness. The more you know your partner, the more you will truly love them, and the more enjoyment you will naturally have. Anything else you see in your partner are self-judgements projected out on them.

Never quit dating. Take time for yourself and your partner. Renew yourself and your relationship, and keep moving forward. Do something different, something creative, something that you would really enjoy. Make a date today.

308

Unhappiness or any area of non-success is a form of revenge on your parents, in spite of what we may say on the surface.

If you are unhappy, you are saying to the world, "My parents did not raise me right." By going around in life with your sad face, you are saying, "Look at what you did to me, Mum and Dad. Because you failed, I am screwed up." But by hurting yourself to get back at your parents, you are cutting off your nose to spite your face.

You and your parents are on the same team. If they failed, it can only be because you have also. So, stop living in the past. To let your happiness rely on the behaviour of others will only bring you suffering. Your forgiveness will free all of you from the past.

Maybe it is time to choose a more mature and self-empowering attitude, one that moves you forward. Maybe it is time to give your parents your happiness – which would move their life forward as well as yourself. The best gifts you can give yourself are the ones you can give them also. Happiness is the best policy for all concerned.

309 **True abundance is not having winners and losers, only winners.**

If you have winners and losers in a situation, the communication has not come to full fruition. There are still areas of hurt and fear, and a fight is still going on at some level. When you have losers, your belief in scarcity is reinforced. So, do not stop the communication until there are only winners.

Do not adjust to pain. Continue any communication until both sides feel as if they have won, and there are only winners.

310 To be yourself is to be a star.

A star is a person who shines so brightly, who gives their gifts so fully, who loves so completely that everyone is drawn by the light of this star to find the way home. For you to truly know yourself, know that you are a star. For you to truly be yourself, recognise the genius in you. Know what a gift you are to everyone around you. A star may do very quiet things – but they shine an intense love-light that burns through the darkness.

Today, recognise yourself as a star, and allow to fall away anything that stops you from shining. Choose to forgive or let go of any grievance or judgement that allows you control over yourself, others, or the situation. Choose not to use anyone or anything to hold yourself back. Choose to utterly and completely love. Nothing else will satisfy you. Nothing else is worthy of you.

311 All pain is the result of misunderstanding.

Suffering means there is something you do not understand. A full understanding heals all of the needs that result in pain, and allows you to move through the resistance that pain is. Wherever you have stopped and refused to go on is an area of pain, fear, and unmet needs. But understanding allows the process to unfold, the fear to be overcome, and the needs met so that you are naturally in rapport with the people around you.

Go into rapport with the people around you. Join them. This allows the understanding that heals pain, fear and needs.

312 **If you join with someone who is attacking you, there is no resistance and nothing to attack.**

Defence creates attack because the defence is a kind of chip on your shoulder that just begs to be knocked off. Any pain inside us calls to other pain. Violence, conscious, or unconscious, on the inside calls for violence on the outside to come toward us. But if you join with the person attacking you, the attack in them deflates. Any attack that comes toward you is a specific call to you for help. Somewhere, deep inside, they believe you might be the person who could help them. Of course they have resistance to that too, a fight against it. They feel almost angry at their attraction to you, and sometimes that ambivalence creates attack. But if you respond with closeness, awareness, and nurturing, the fight can end, and both of you can move forward to a new level.

Move toward someone attacking you. Call them. Write them. Send them love. If no one is attacking you now, go back to the past where you have been attacked, and recreate the scene in your imagination. Find someone who is in disagreement with you or criticising you or attacking you, and move out to support them.

313 Having it all is the promise a relationship brings.

It is important to know that we can have it all. Adjusting to limitations, giving up on having true abundance, or having everything work in your life is not a sign of maturity. A relationship can create the inspiration for you to keep moving past your limitations. The love within a relationship can move you past the deadness and conflicts to higher and higher levels. Each problem you transcend, each temptation that you bypass, brings you to a new level where you, your relationship, and your whole life becomes more abundant. The promise of the relationship is that as it keeps unfolding, you keep unfolding, and more and more grace comes to you and fills your life.

Relax and imagine that you are standing with your partner, and all of a sudden, you begin sinking down into the ground past all the conflicts and all the deadness. Imagine that the two of you keep sinking through the ground until you get to a more essential place. Whether this place is a meadow, an open space, or a place of light, just feel yourself knowing the true essence of the relationship and its possibility, and know that this movement – through all of the misunderstandings – is leading you toward having it all.

314 The competition in your present relationship began in the family in which you grew up.

All families, no matter how healthy, contain subtle, or not-so-subtle aspects of competition. This shows especially if there was any kind of scarcity – not enough money or love to go around, or not enough of a balance so that everyone got to enjoy the others fully. The competition that you now face is something that began a long time ago with the taking on of your personalities.

Your personalities are all built on a sense of comparison: "Don't I deserve love?" And therefore, "Don't I deserve love a little bit more than my brother or sister or anybody else?" Now, these aspects are so much a part of us that they are like a skintight body stocking. Every personality marks a place where we gave up a gift in ourselves to gain everybody else's approval and to feel included. But personality is like a cellophane wrapper between other people and you. It keeps you from receiving. It keeps you self-conscious. It prevents you from reaching out to people and being expanded, spontaneous, outrageous and fun.

Look at the competition in your life and where it began a long time ago. You can re-balance the past. Realise that there is enough for everyone in your present relationship.

The enemies that seem to have sprung up in my family I will now see as my allies, because the more they succeed, the more I succeed. The more my partner succeeds, the more I succeed. I will reach beyond competition and support my partner. I will see their true self. When I feel self-conscious or self-tortured or caught by the voice of distraction in my head, I will reach out to someone else, and we will both be free.

315 What you are expecting of another is what you are not giving to them.

All expectations come out of demands, which come out of fear that we might not have what we need. That is why you demand it rather than ask for it. But your fear that they might not give it to you, actually, stems from your not giving it to them.

You could turn your expectation into an invitation (which is much more naturally responded to) just by being willing to give the very thing that you are expecting from your partner or those around you.

Where do you feel unrequited? Look at the expectation you may have of someone, whether it is your partner, your parent, your child, your boss – whomever it may be. If you expect anything of them, feel yourself giving them the very thing you would like to have from them. You will soon find a natural giving and receiving between the two of you.

316 **The helper role allows you to feel superior while being afraid of an equal partner.**

That is why it is a role. The role, as a compensation, covers up a feeling of inferiority, of not being good enough, of not being worthy enough. So we tend to choose someone who can be co-dependant with us, someone who is really afraid of moving on also. We move into collusion in a relationship to hold ourselves back with one person being the identified problem person. Another aspect of the helper role is when we help someone improve to the point of being in an equal-level relationship with us, just at that point we push them away, and they move on leaving us empty-handed. We are afraid to stand as an equal partner because we are afraid of getting hurt. We feel we are not worthy to have the relationship succeed, or that we have enough power or confidence to handle an equal partner.

Look at all the times in your life when you have chosen someone in order to be the helper. Was it so that you both would not move forward? Or did you see the potential in them, and when they got to a place of healing and equality, you pushed them away? Whatever your situation, be willing to be equal, to share your feelings, and even to share your experiences of not feeling quite adequate. Let go of your role, and step forward in your life by allowing for your happiness. If you allow yourself to receive, and your partner to become your equal, you bless yourself as much as you are blessing them.

317 The truth creates abundance.

What is experienced but not said can hold you back in a relationship. Without communication, there is no joining, and you cannot move forward. The truth creates a line of connection. But when you are afraid to tell something to your partner, what you withhold (your feelings, or something that needs to be handled, or something that has happened) creates a certain blockage between your partner and you, and deadness in your relationship. It is your level of connection with your partner that will generate true abundance – not just money, but joy, happiness, creativity and all of the good things of life.

Your truth creates abundance. Find out where you are withholding yourself. What you are withholding may not be true, but it is the truth of your experience at this point. Once you finish sharing it, you can integrate it into the relationship, and you can both move forward.

318 If you do not have something in your life, it is because you have been in control.

You do not control the wave you are surfing or conquer the mountain you are skiing. You go with the flow of it. And to the extent you do, you become successful. Your control says you think you have a better answer not only for yourself, but for anyone else who would care to listen. What it hides is your fear of loss, getting hurt, or having it be so good you might be overwhelmed. In fact, you would rather not have it be good than be overwhelmed, or have to deal with old pain that may or may not be there. Thus, your control stands in the way of success.

The highest level of success is something you flow with, not something planned. Be willing to give up your control and see what answer life wants to show you. Imagine that you do not have to make the dawn come up every morning, that you do not have to push the river. Imagine that the universe is running just perfectly, and everything is moving toward success if you would just get out of the way. Use your trust to know that everything is coming your way. Put your future in the hands of your Higher Mind.

319 No matter what your pain, giving creates healing.

Are you feeling numb? Are you feeling "blah"? Are you feeling self-tortured, self-conscious, ashamed, embarrassed, hurt, jealous, afraid, in despair, empty, useless, futile or lost? If you chose to totally give yourself through any of these feelings or be in service, you would create breakthrough. Where you give, you create your birth. You move out of deadness and into the flow. You move out of self-consciousness and self-torture, and into grace. True giving brings about receiving, and is one of the greatest healers in the world.

Look at where giving would improve the situation, where you could reach out to other people to make things better. Do it now.

320 **Power struggle is a demand of the other to meet needs, which could be fulfilled for you and your partner by you simply taking the next step.**

In a power struggle, we think the other person is somehow the source of our receiving. They are the ones who should make us happy. So we fight with them to do it our way to meet our needs. But fighting with your partner is just a way of delaying yourself from moving forward in your life, which could create the fulfilment of your needs and those of your partner also.

Close your eyes, relax, and ask that the next step come to you. Say yes to whatever is coming in your life, knowing that it will contain the answers to what is plaguing you now. Just say yes. Be willing to be open to whatever it is; to be taught about how the situation could become the very best; to move off your position and have it be different for you and your partner.

321 When you want to have a need fulfilled, let go.

Needs are spoken or unspoken demands. Whether you are aware of them or not, they create a resistance to your receiving. No need comes from outside yourself. They are things we think we need when we do not recognise our true wholeness.

Let go of your needs. Close your eyes and imagine sinking down within yourself until you come to a place of total wholeness for yourself, a place of no needs. Or imagine that you move forward in time, even beyond this life, to a place of great creativity where you are totally whole. Here, you will find that your needs are naturally released, and that the wholeness is actually the most essential part of you. But in our everyday life, where we rush around trying to get all of the things we think we need, we forget that on the very deepest level, our needs are an illusion and our wholeness is the essential reality of our mind.

322 Every blessing you give blesses you.

Whenever you wish someone the best or give someone love, you feel good. Every time you help someone, the help you give and the healing they reach gets added to your life.

Close your eyes and allow to come to your mind people who need your blessing, who need your love sent to them. They need the power of your mind added to their life. As you give to them, feel how good you feel. Know that your giving multiplies the power of your blessing. Throughout the day, any time you meet someone – people on the street, people you pass by, people at work – just bless them.

323 The more you give of yourself to another, the more you see who they are.

But criticism limits your ability to see and understand them. The German poet Rainer Marie Rilke says that we can only approach a work of art through love. How much truer this is when we approach a human being. If we bring the love that allows us to understand, worlds upon worlds are open to us of the mystery that they are. The more love you bring to the person you are with, the more you feel naturally inspired to support and enjoy who they are. If you are not enjoying someone, it is because you are not giving to them. The more you give to anyone, the more you get to enjoy yourself. This is not true of sacrifice, so it is easy to see when you have counterfeit giving going on.

Look at some of the significant people in your life that you are not enjoying. Now is the time to reach out to them, to extend yourself more until you get to the point of enjoying them. You will find how much you have removed yourself from some of them. Just give and give and give until you get to see their beauty, and how much fun it is to be with them.

324 If you see a problem, it is your problem, and you are called upon to do something about it.

Denial will not help you here because the problem will affect you whether you accept it or not. Being able to see the snake in the grass does not mean that it will not affect you if you step on it. If you see a job that needs to be done, you need to respond to it in order to make it better. Recognise that what you see is what you are called upon to take care of.

As you expand your awareness, you expand your flow. People who want to help will see and hear the calls for help all around them. Your willingness to respond to these calls will move you forward. You will find your natural place as the focal point of healing, and as the leader in the situation to make everything better. You can do this and still live your own life.

Look out at your world, and see who really needs help. What is the problem that you could respond to or make better? Respond now.

325 Your self-concepts are killing you.

We all want to have a good self-concept because we think this naturally makes us feel better. But self-concepts stem from doubts we have about ourselves as negative and bad. So we have a whole layer of all these good things we think about ourselves, which are merely compensations. If you were to pierce this layer, you would find a garbage bin of negative self-concepts deep in the subconscious and even the unconscious mind. In fact, if we really knew what we thought about ourselves, we would probably not be able to stand it. The good news is that these negative self-concepts are not true either.

Every thought we have about ourselves is not the truth, because it is just a thought. Every self-concept is something you are trying to prove – which you do not really believe or you would have no need to prove it. Unless it is meditative or creative, thinking is always one step after the event, and is, in effect, a form of resistance and control. But your essence is something much more whole that never really needs questioning. When you pass by the self-concepts, you reach a new depth where you find positive beliefs about yourself, beliefs that are not merely compensations. This is the realm just before you hit bliss and ecstasy, the area just before enlightenment. It is the doorway to seeing things as they really are.

Today, be willing to move through any self-concept, positive or negative, so you can reach the knowledge of your essence and wholeness. You will know when you are getting there because you will feel joyful and good about yourself. You will feel how much you are loved, and how much you love. You will feel your natural creativity. Let go of all your self-concepts. They are robbing you of you.

326 Everything that happens in your life is a communication to a significant other.

Everything that happens to you, and that you have done in life is a communication. Look at the mishaps in your life, and ask yourself, "Who was I communicating to, and what was the message I was giving?" If you are willing to really look, you will see that you are always giving a message to yourself, to God, to your parents, to your significant other, even ex-significant others, and to anyone else who truly happens to be in the situation. But subconscious communication has much less of a chance for success. The mishap has occurred in the first place because we are so frightened of communication that we would rather have something happen to us than to be in touch with ourselves and communicate directly to the other person. Sometimes you will find that having negative things happen to you is a way of getting back at others; sometimes, it is a call for help on your part; other times, it is actually a way of telling someone you love them. But this is pure sacrifice, and it is really harmful to your own life. There is some major misunderstanding between you and the other person if you sacrifice yourself to get their love or approval.

Choose three major experiences in your life. Ask yourself what you are or were communicating to the significant people there. As you understand what messages you were giving, you will begin to understand what was going on with you that you would create such an event in your life. Learning to make your subconscious communication conscious allows you much greater success in your life. Bringing what is in the darkness into the light creates healing.

327 If you do not trust, you do not love.

In fact, you do not even trust yourself because to the extent you can trust yourself, you can trust another. So, something else is going on, which is probably some form of control. If you are not trusting someone, you may be feeling a need that makes them attractive to you; or you may be feeling desire for this person in some way – but you are not feeling love.

Trust is the power of your mind being given to another person to support them toward integrity and truth. So give this most vital factor that goes hand-in-hand with love.

Today, give trust to your partner and to anyone around you who really deserves it. It is the best gift that you can give to your partner today, because there is no problem that trust could not heal. It is a transformational tool, which makes the situation safe, and empowers you. At the same time, know that naiveté is not trust; your instincts will tell you what is. If you have the confidence, if you really trust yourself and your own personal power, you can trust anyone.

328 It is only through commitment that you receive.

Many people feel there is no life after commitment. What they are talking about is not commitment, but some form of contraction, sacrifice, or holding themselves back. Perhaps they are remembering a time when they were love-slaves, or did things to win approval. This is especially true of independent people: to the extent that people are independent, they are afraid about going into sacrifice again. But neither your independence nor your sacrifice has anything to do with commitment.

Your commitment is your choice to give yourself fully in every way you know how. As you do, you naturally receive more. Commitment means "to send with". And your willingness to send yourself to someone, to commit yourself, allows you to receive from them.

Realise where you may have a lack of commitment because you have misunderstood it as a form of sacrifice. Be willing to let all of that sacrifice go. Know that you can make truer choices now, that you can give yourself truly, and that you do not have to be afraid of being captured. You can speak the truth so as not to be used. Today, allow yourself to acknowledge where you are afraid, and make the choice to give yourself so you can succeed.

329 Love comes towards us all the time.

But it is our lack of vision and awareness that does not allow us to receive it. Our judgements and grievances create a bad feeling about ourselves, which does not allow us to see that all good things are moving toward us if we would just open our eyes and receive them.

Imagine you are in your very favourite place, and that all the love your family has ever had for you is coming toward you. Now, imagine that all the love of anyone who has ever believed in you – teachers, friends, co-workers, mentors, creative colleagues – is coming toward you. Then, see the love of your spiritual teacher coming to you. And now feel the love of God that is always coming to you. Just allow yourself to see and receive all this love. It is a great day for feeling how much you are loved at every moment.

330 If anyone is the bad guy, we all lose.

Whenever we judge someone to be the bad guy, we go into power struggle with them. We avoid them or attack them, even if only in our mind. We set up a struggle in which we are trying not to be affected by them, or we are trying to beat them. But where anyone loses, we have all lost. We have created a situation where somebody has to pay the bill. Guess who it is going to be? So be willing to look beyond "good guys" and "bad guys". This judgement is actually just a way of hiding things that need to be handled or communicated. If you are willing to understand and move beyond your competition, there is a place, paradoxically enough, where both of you could be satisfied – now and in the future.

Close your eyes, relax, and think of the person you are judging today. Somebody is wrong, somebody is the bad guy. Ask the part of your mind that has all the answers to take care of this problem and to show you that paradoxical way that everyone can win, not only now, but throughout eternity. Do not stop until everyone can win.

331 **Commitment can come only out of self-valuing.**

The reason we have such a hard time with commitment and do not think we could last for the long haul, is that we do not think anyone, including ourselves, is worth that kind of continuous giving. We do not value ourselves, so we do not value other people. To the extent we do not value ourselves, we will find ourselves locked up in roles, duties and rules, doing the right things for the wrong reasons. But there is a place of greater responsiveness, of truer choice, of higher ethics and that comes with commitment.

Today, you are asked to value yourself and to really give to yourself. As you learn to value yourself, you will see a constant unfolding that can happen with you and with others.

332 **Letting someone abuse you is not a service to anyone.**

Respect yourself, and ask for self-respect from those around you. Prevent people from harming you, because later, their guilt will create a vicious cycle of either withdrawal or recurrent attacks. Sometimes the ego puts us in a situation where we get abused, and we let it happen because of our concepts of non-violence, or feelings of weakness. We put ourselves in abusive situations because in some ways we feel guilty, or feel a need to sacrifice.

In any situation in which you may be feeling emotionally or even physically abused, do not allow it, for it will not help anyone. Do what it takes to prevent the other person from abusing you. Sometimes you need to communicate very strongly with them. Or, you may need to remove yourself from the situation because of the nature of the event. If you do remove yourself – but keep pouring love and support toward that person – the situation will begin unfolding for you.

Every form of abuse is a place we get others to punish us for subconscious guilt. But if you are willing to explore the guilt you are feeling that is creating the situation, you can change it instantly. Ask yourself: If I were to know, at what age did this guilt spring up? Then ask, who else was involved? and what was the guilt about? Remember, guilt is a mistake. It is a decision you made about yourself, which you can resolve and heal. In whatever situation you were in, you left your centre. So, ask your Higher Mind to carry you back to your centre, and from there, to help you extend the light within you to pull everyone back to their centre. Notice how good all of you feel at this point. Now feel how this affects your present situation.

333 We are doing the best we can, given our inner and outer circumstances.

When you do not understand why someone is acting a certain way, ask yourself, "What would I have to be feeling to be acting in that way?" People behave according to the way they feel, and what we feel comes from what we believe, value, or think. These are the products of the different experiences and choices we have made in our lives. Realise that, given what has been going on with us, we are doing the very best we can. Knowing this, we can have understanding and compassion for ourselves and other people in the human condition.

Close your eyes, and allow yourself to go back to a situation where you made a major decision against yourself and your life. Who was in that situation with you? What were they doing? What must they have been feeling to act the way they did? In any kind of traumatic situation, everybody is acting differently but feeling the same way. You know how painful that situation has been for you. Everyone in it was feeling the same way underneath, or it could not have come about in that way.

When you reach that feeling, you can have a sense of compassion for yourself and everyone there. You can make another decision about yourself and your life. In that imagined situation, realise their behaviour was a call for love. Feel your light reaching out and connecting with everyone there. Notice as the connection occurs, how the pain and conflict seem to fall away for everyone.

334 Pain can be an excellent teacher.

Do not try to run away from pain, because when you avoid it, you avoid certain lessons. Be willing to have the courage to feel the pain through, to see what it can teach you and give to you. While pain can be healed instantly it still takes a willingness to face it. Once you feel it completely through, it will disappear. Your willingness to take this new attitude toward pain will then allow you to move into certain situations that you would otherwise avoid, and to see the resolution of situations where you would otherwise create attack or avoidance. Once you stop resisting pain, you can begin to find true and quick ways through.

Be willing to face the feelings that are inside you and those coming toward you. You can use pain as your teacher, and it will be a kind teacher if you do not resist it. Your willingness will give you a certain responsiveness and strength that seems missing right now.

335 Ego is everything this side of oneness.

Oneness works through cooperation, connection, and mutual support. But the ego is out for itself, hoarding its little bit to feed its own needs, insisting on separateness and having more than anyone else in certain areas. The extent of your separateness is the extent to which you feel pain, experience problems, or feel needs. Your ego has you doing many useless tasks to create security for yourself and to build up your self-concepts. But all of this is a waste of time, because who you are does not need to be built up. Who you are is more essential than that, more whole than that.

Allow yourself to move toward people today, and to join them. See the areas where you are keeping yourself separate, and realise that separation is totally unnecessary. Your communication and your willingness to join and cooperate create a new level of partnership where you get to experience the joys of oneness, abundance, love, happiness and creativity.

336

If you don't accept where you are, you cannot expect to move ahead.

When you are in a very difficult situation, and you are resisting and rejecting it, you get stuck. Conversely, as soon as you accept what you are experiencing, you are able to move to the next step. For example, imagine being caught in a riptide, and you are fighting against it, trying to swim out of it. Doing this would just wear you out until you drowned. But if you would just relax and let the riptide carry you, it would swing you in a greater and greater arc until finally it would carry you beyond it. At that point, you could swim away freely.

If you find that you are trying to accept a situation so as to be released, but you are not moving forward, it may be that you have adjusted or adapted to the situation. This is just a form of sacrifice and compromise where you feel you have lost. Why adapt to something that is not true? Do not compromise – communicate. Do not adjust – resolve. Do not resist – accept.

Be willing to accept any difficult situation you are in, and feel yourself moving through it. Today, instead of judgement, use acceptance in any situation you encounter.

337 Guilt insists on punishment, but mistakes call only for correction.

When we feel guilty, we create punishment for ourselves to get rid of the bad feeling. Then after the punishment, we feel okay about ourselves for a while. But situations that punish us make us feel bad, and not only reinforce the self-concept of guilt (which is not true), but increase it. Further, when you feel badly, you act badly, using withdrawal or aggressiveness; this in turn creates another attack that keeps the vicious cycle of guilt going.

Sometimes you see this in a child's behaviour; they feel so bad about themselves that they have to behave so as to bring on some form of punishment. Once that happens, they feel settled and calm. However, by punishing the child, you may "win the battle but lose the war" because this type of behaviour towards a child will beat into them the very thing that you are trying to prevent. Similarly, as adults we call in all kinds of things to punish ourselves: physical illnesses, accidents, mishaps, failures, lack of money – paradoxically reinforcing the guilt we are trying to get rid of.

When we feel guilty, we beat ourselves up, just as when we feel we have sinned, we beat ourselves up with guilt and retribution. Thus, we attach sin to guilt instead of learning the lesson at hand. Yet the word "sin" actually comes from an old Greek Archery term meaning, to miss the mark. Sin then, is just a mistake. Once we realise this, we can learn the lesson, correct the mistake, and let go of the guilt.

Let go of all the things you are feeling bad about so that you can learn the lesson. Your willingness to learn is the easiest way and it releases the bad feeling of self-punishment. Guilt refuses to learn the lesson, so the problem keeps getting repeated. Guilt is an idea about ourselves we have made up. It is ego-generated to keep us locked into certain self-concepts. Since guilt is untrue, it can be simply let go of today and everyday.

an area that is a catch-all for all of the misunderstandings, grievances, and missed connections. Anything that needs to be taken care of will show up in this area. It could be communication, money, sex, lack of success, health problems – anything can be the symptom for all the problems of the relationship. So whatever that chronic problem is in your relationship, do not despair. Just realise that every relationship chooses one area to be the closet for unfinished business. Be willing to attend to this area, but recognise that it is just a symptom of many areas of disconnection in your relationship. As you connect with your partner, you will find even this chronic area gradually improving.

Realise what the chronic problem is. Imagine it standing between you and your partner. Now see, coming from your heart, a beam of light and love that passes right through that chronic problem and connects with your partner's heart. Feel this draw you together. Now imagine a light passing from your head through the problem to connect with your partner's head. Repeat this exercise with your and your partner's throat, your genitals, your stomachs, your abdomens, and the base of your spines. As those lights shine through the problems, you are able to step through the problem to hold each other. As you do, just feel yourself melting into your partner, and your partner melt into you. What emerges from this will be the next step.

339 Permission blesses your partner and those around you.

Permission is an act of leadership. It is a certain, natural place of authority you reach by transcending your personality, by shifting from a place of self-restriction, to finding spontaneity and responsiveness. When we come into a relationship, we have certain areas of giftedness where we have already given permission to ourselves. So we can naturally give our partner permission to receive in this area when they are in conflict; we do this through the authority vested in us by the truth and our own growth. We can give support and invite them to a new place of understanding and consciousness. Giving permission is one of the easiest ways to free someone who may have locked themselves up. It blesses your partner and those around you in areas where they have reached places of leadership.

Look around you. What permission would you like to give to your partner? What permission would you like to give to those who associate with you today? The more you give this permission, the more you free them, winning their support and gratitude.

340 You do not have to do anything for God except remember Heaven.

The best gift you could give to God is to remember your home. Your home is a place of happiness, no matter what experience is occurring. Let's say you are in a very difficult situation, and you begin to remember Heaven; or to use another metaphor you begin to remember total happiness and choose to experience that. Remembering Heaven at the point of difficulty begins to move the situation forward. It sets up a resonance in all of your brothers and sisters and in everyone you love, so that everything that is not happiness, is just an illusion and will, at some point, fall away. The more you remember Heaven, the more you will bring Heaven to earth. You do not have to do anything for God, necessarily. You do not have to lead crusades, or accomplish major projects. All you have to do is remember the love and happiness that is Heaven. As you do in each situation, everyone is freed, beginning with yourself.

Today, remember Heaven. Write it on your refrigerator, your bathroom wall, your place of work, so there is something that catches your attention to remember to be happy, to remember Heaven, to remember that no matter what is going on, you can choose to change it by choosing Heaven. You do not have to be a martyr for God. Why would the highest force in the universe need your blood and your suffering? When we think God is asking us to suffer, this is our projection on God, our way of making God small. The verse, "Vengeance is Mine sayeth the Lord," (The Bible) does not mean that God is going to be vengeful against us. It means that God wants us to give up our vengeance to Him. Our projection of God reflects our guilt and our belief that

God is going to get us. That is why we punish ourselves and go into sacrifice so often. We are saying, “God, don’t bother to get me – I’m already punishing myself. Look at how bad I’m hurting. Aren’t I a good person?” But all we really need to do is just receive God’s love and be happy – to remember Heaven, our home. Somebody today can be really helped by your joy. Spread Heaven by remembering it.

341 Every relationship has a purpose.

Just as each person has a personal purpose, so does each relationship. Its purpose is to create and experience happiness. Where there is unhappiness, the purpose is healing, which is always concerned with some form of forgiveness, of giving where we have withdrawn. But more specifically, each relationship, if it reaches its true partnership and creativity, will have a personal function that allows more creativity to come into the world. Sometimes this will be in the form of children, creative projects, or a level of consciousness that each person attains as a result of the relationship. It may be the inspiration your relationship provides as a healing factor to all the people around you, letting them know there is hope for relationships, that we can be ourselves and still have love.

What is the purpose of your relationship? By your coming together, what has your relationship come to give the world? Out of the love of the two of you, there will be a gift to the world.

342 Whatever abundance you allow yourself to receive, you naturally give to your partner.

In any relationship you will have areas of accomplishment which your partner has not yet achieved; it may be in areas of expertise or in areas where you fully give yourself. As a result of this giving and creativity, a natural abundance comes back to you. As you receive this, you naturally have a gift for your partner. Whatever particular talent or gift resonates in you will begin to resonate in them by your closeness and intimacy. They will discover that they have certain talents that they did not know they had.

The extent of your joining is the extent to which they will naturally begin to act out this particular gift or talent and receive it on their own. Both of you bring gifts to the relationship, and this abundance is what you give to make the relationship grow.

See what you have that is a gift for your partner. If you have been complaining that they are not giving you a certain thing, this is exactly what you have enough of for both of you. As you provide this gift until it is accomplished for both partners, you will find yourself satisfied. From this new level of partnership, there will be sharing and new gifts for both of you.

343 If you do not feel, you die.

Without feeling, we cannot feel alive, or feel joy, or feel enough to know that we are in pain and need to change what we are doing. But most of all, our feelings help us to find what is meaningful. Meaning goes along with feeling. It gives us direction and purpose. When we are fulfilling our purpose and living out of true meaning, we are living Heaven's meaning rather than the useless little jobs we make for ourselves. In this we find a state of joy, love and creativity. So it is important to feel as much as we can, to expand ourselves. What is negative can be felt and let go of easily if we choose. What feels painful can be there as our barometer, indicating the need to change some choice in our life.

Today is a day to give up being one of God's frozen people. Allow yourself to really feel. Allow your feelings to direct you to all the states of love, joy, fun and happiness. If there is a bad feeling, feel it until it is gone, or make the change necessary. Really allow yourself to feel good today. Learn how to say, "Aaaaaah!" about life and the situation you are in today.

344

Fear is the basic emotion under any negative experience.

The answers and natural responses to end this fear are: loving, forgiving, supporting, giving, trusting, asking for Heaven's help. Each one of these create confidence, letting go, accepting, understanding. And all have a way of moving through fear. If you are wondering what is going on in any negative situation, ask yourself what you are afraid of, what you are afraid you will lose.

Write down three negative experiences, or situations that are less than great in your life. Then feel the situation to see what you are afraid of, and write that down beside each experience. Now, write down the antidote, the form of responsiveness that pops into your mind that would heal this fear. Whatever answer comes up, apply it to the situation. Even in the most difficult situations, you will find yourself moving out of your fear and moving forward.

345 Essence is always attractive.

Your essence is the part of you that is not looking for anyone else's approval. Essence does not create a personality for itself, or go into sacrifice to be included. Your essence is something that is so attractive that it shines out from you and creates your beauty. It is spontaneous, intuitive, fun, and rascally. People love this energy when it flows. It doesn't matter who you are, it just matters that you let your essence out. It creates charisma. It creates a field of influence around you, and an aura around you. It creates the excitement, the stimulation, the electricity around you.

Being in your essence is a natural form of leadership. When you have integrity and are acting from your essence, you allow people to come to you; and you are able to move in creative ways toward that sense of true joining that does not ask people to give up their gifts to be part of the crowd. Essence is always attractive and confirming, and it makes people feel good.

Stop doing all the things you think people are demanding of you. Stop acting in all those nice little ways that personality asks you to act. Just come from your essence today, shine out today and really have a good time.

346 A lack of money means a lack of giving and receiving in the relationship.

How much warm, soft cash do you have in your relationship? Relationships can generate abundance, but that has to do with the amount of giving and receiving within them. Where there is a money problem, there is an energy problem in the relationship. Maybe you are caught up in a power struggle, a form of revenge, in roles and duties, or guilt. But none of these are real giving and receiving.

To shift out of your money problem, tell the truth, and move into true giving and receiving. Make true contact with your partner. You will love it not only for the intimacy, joy and good feelings, but because there will be a lot more money to support the creativity in your relationship.

347 Seeing God in everything and all situations allows love to take you home.

You will know that life is being taken care of for you. Your vision allows you to see the love in everything and how much you are loved. When you see this, you do not have to work so hard; you can just allow yourself to receive. Seeing God in everything and all situations draws you towards a state of Heaven, ecstasy, bliss. You can feel the joyful understanding that God loves you a million times more than you know. God is in everything, totally surrounding you with this love. If you knew that, you would get out of your own way, you would release your pain and your mistaken self-concepts, and you would feel yourself drawn toward all that love. You would be willing to bring Heaven to earth.

See God in everything and in all situations today. See God in the eyes of your children, in the eyes of your co-workers, and in the eyes of your partner.

348 Appreciation moves us out of comparison and envy.

Comparison is always a way of feeling pain, now or in the future. We may feel better than someone else today, but it is only a matter of time before we meet someone ahead of us. We compare because we are hoping we will find ourselves a little bit better and therefore a little bit more deserving of love. But we could know that we are deserving of love now.

Envy is a feeling that gets us completely stuck. We see someone as better than we are, so we envy what they have, not recognising that what we see in them is also within us – or else we could not perceive it. Our appreciation allows us to heal envy and move forward because it allows us to enjoy their gifts. As we enjoy their gifts, we receive them. As we receive them, the energy within us resonates with those gifts, and begins to unfold. Your willingness to be in service to people you envy, which is a form of giving out of deep appreciation for them, allows you to develop those gifts that you see in them in the quickest possible way.

Recognise that appreciation is a gift to you and to everyone around you. Appreciation creates flow in which you move forward and feel blessed by the people and gifts around you, because what they have, you can enjoy too. And as you enjoy their gift, you will feel it emerging in you.

349 When you do not feel understood, it is because you do not understand.

Many of us come out of childhood feeling as if we are not understood, or we are in a present relationship in which we are not feeling understood. But if you look deeper at your childhood or at your present relationship, you would realise that you could only be feeling this way if you do not understand what was happening with your parents or what is happening now with your present partner. So take a deeper look. People act a certain way because of how they feel. They are sometimes so caught up in their own pain that they do not have the power, energy, or time to be able to focus on you and see what you need. But your understanding of the situation creates the healing of your own needs. Understanding releases you, releases fear and transforms separation to connectedness.

Look at situations in which you feel misunderstood by people in your life, and ask yourself, "What don't I understand about them?" As you raise your understanding of what was going on in those situations, or what is going on now, you will find that you have a natural sense of being understood.

350 When the receiver is ready, the gift appears.

This is just one more secret to help remind you that you are in charge of your world, that you are not stuck with what does not come to you. When you are ready to receive, the gift appears. Now, what would it take for you to prepare yourself to receive the gifts that you would like in your life? Certainly, it would mean getting over fear. And it would mean having a sense of worthiness. So get ready to receive. All of the things you think you want – open yourself up to receiving them. Know yourself as worthy. Ask for the grace to transcend the fear or self-concepts that keep you away from what is waiting for your readiness.

Do what you intuitively do on the inside to allow yourself to be ready to receive the gifts you wish. What holds you back from receiving? What could you allow yourself to choose, or do, that would assist you to open your heart for the gift that is coming to you now?

351 Complaining is inferiority in the form of arrogance.

Your complaining comes out of a sense of inferiority, a sense that you do not have much power in the situation. Yet it takes the form of arrogance. You feel above the situation, as if this should not be happening to you. Your complaint is a verbal or mental attack on the situation around you. In your arrogance, you expect things to change, but you are the one being asked to change. You could change easily to feel better about yourself, by giving yourself some recognition, value, and respect. And as you change in this inner way, the outside situation begins to reflect the change.

Take a close look at yourself. Where are you complaining to yourself? These are areas where you are reinforcing a sense of inferiority. Take a step forward, or choose to value yourself more. Either one will begin to change the situation in which you feel stuck.

352 Unless you become like a little child, you cannot enter the Kingdom of Heaven.

The key here is not to become childish, but to become child-like. This is not a state of immaturity; it is actually the only true reality about our connection with God. A child lives a simple life, which allows the mind to focus. Children are open to all that comes toward them. Children are innocent, and feel worthy. They look to their parents knowing they will be given all good things. In the same way, we, in innocence could look to our God and the world around us with expectancy, knowing that all good things are coming our way. As we open ourselves, as we let go of the thought that we have to carry and do everything, that we have to make it all better, we take a natural delight and a natural humour in the situation that surrounds us.

Today, let go of all the cares and worries you have, all the sense of duty, and everything you feel you have to do. Imagine that you could live a very simple life. It would just be a life of love, a life of enjoyment. This is the life of the child, the life of a master. Ask yourself, "What will come to me today? What will happen? What gifts will I receive? What am I called to today?"

353 Love allows you to get out of your own way.

Your ego is the calcified belief in your separation. It separates you from others and from communication with God. Your ego is your fear and insecurity. The more your fear and insecurity is out in the world, the more it sets up barriers to your success, which, at some level, is what the ego wishes. It wishes you to be delayed because it wants you to think that you need it. But the ego is a very small aspect of our mind trying to act as if it is totally needed.

Love allows us to get out of our own way. Love allows us to transcend this fear and these calcified ways of reacting. Love allows us to freely receive. Love raises us above the worries and cares, and creates responsiveness that brings contact and joy. Love communicates, extends itself and plays.

Today, go beyond your ego and separateness. Get out of your own way. Love everyone you meet.

354 **Sacrifice is based on a vicious circle of superiority and inferiority.**

When we are sacrificing, when we are taking care of others in the untrue helper role, we feel above them. We feel as if we are just a little bit better. But in truth, we actually feel inferior, and we do not feel up to going out without protection. We feel we need a role to raise us above the situation, which is what we did to get this sacrifice started.

We were in a situation where we were experiencing loss, and rather than experience it, we backed away because it felt like it was too much of us. So we took on the role of helping the people around us to avoid our loss, which, ironically, just got us stuck in it. We have not completed the mourning; we have not gotten over the loss. So now, as a result of defending ourselves against feeling this old loss and present losses, we have thrown ourselves into situations where we can feel either above or below people. But this inferiority, this old pain, creates a situation that blocks us from receiving, and wears us down.

Look at any area where you may be feeling yourself a little bit above, where you are condescending to help. Or look at where you feel below, where you feel other people need to be helping you, or taking care of you. Either way, you do not feel good enough to be their partner. You are in a situation of sacrifice, and doing anything you think they want.

Now allow yourself to go back to the time and place of that original unmourned situation, and ask for Heaven's help. Give to everyone in the situation, allowing love and grace to pour through you, filling everyone there. This can release the present situation of sacrifice, and allow you to move forward to more equal partnerships in your life.

355 Deadness in sex or in your relationship can be healed by balanced relatedness to your family.

Most of the time, the root of the deadness has to do with our relationship with our parent of the opposite sex (sometimes, even the same sex). There may have been some form of competition, or lack of closeness and love where we lost our bonding. If we are fused with that parent, at some point we will come to a place of burn-out because we feel as if we have sacrificed too much. Or we will experience repulsion or even revulsion because we feel as if we are too close to that parent, and do not have our own life with our own natural boundaries. So when we go into burn-out because of fusion with our partner which is a carry over from our parents, we have a sense of anger or rage toward them because we are so exhausted. Sometimes we even have a sense of repulsion for them because we do not have a natural understanding of where the boundary is between their life and our life. This is because fusion is counterfeit intimacy, not a place of joining love and the refreshment that comes from such bonding. It is a place that avoids communication.

Our willingness to choose to give to our parents or the siblings with whom we are fused allows that natural balance to occur; this can give life and breath to the counterfeit intimacy and closeness of fusion. And it allows us to live our life in our present relationship, rather than the life we think our parents wanted for us – a life of sacrifice.

Look deeply at your life and ask for Heaven's help in creating the forgiveness and balance in the early situation with your parents and siblings, so that life can be brought into your present relationship. Close your eyes, imagine your early family, and ask your Higher Mind to set up a natural balance and centredness within you, one that ends all competition and fusion.

356 Fun is one of the true forms of responsiveness.

Fun comes from one of the higher states of consciousness. It is an inspired state through which we bring humour and flow into the situation. To bring fun into any situation is to generate more energy of expectancy. Fun has the same dynamics as luck, so when you are having fun, you naturally create more luck. Fun and humour go hand-in-hand. Fun, appreciation, inspiration, spontaneity and naughtiness are all forms of leadership. Fun is true responsiveness.

Today, remember fun, no matter how difficult things are. When things are difficult or serious, they get stuck. Seriousness and heaviness come out of roles and duties. So today, be a leader, and bring fun and humour into any situation. Your naughtiness, your irresistibility, and your fun are great gifts to your partner and to any work situation. Enjoy the dance of fun continuously because, after all, you are not going to take this reality seriously, are you?

357

Whenever you think someone is using you, you are using them to hold yourself back.

When we do not feel that we are someone's natural or equal partner, we give ourselves up to be used. Then, we feel hurt, or feel a great deal of sacrifice. But, in truth, we are using this person. If we were to look fully at the dynamics of the situation in our subconscious mind, we would see that we are using the situation because we were afraid of moving forward and facing intimacy, or ourselves. Our willingness to move forward can totally transform the situation.

When you think someone is using you, realise that you are actually using them to hold you back. Do not be willing to use anyone or anything to hold yourself back. Be willing to move forward, to say yes to that next big step in your life.

358 All problems are a result of feeling separate.

There is only one problem, and that problem creates all problems – the feeling of lack of connection. And out of this lack of connection, a feeling of fear arises. This naturally leads to separate interests and conflict, rather than a commonweal.

Look at the problems you have today, and where you feel disconnected, or from whom you feel disconnected. And then just imagine that you are connected with all of those people, because the truth is that we are all connected. But for various reasons, we create little attack thoughts or grievances that result in the illusion of separation. In reality, we are connected with everyone and everything that is. Just allow yourself to feel your natural connection because it will resolve the problem right now.

359 What you take is what you lose.

This is an interesting dynamic, because the more you take, the emptier you feel, and the more you try to get, the more insecure you feel. Taking is a paradox in which the more you take, the less you are satisfied. This is because taking sets up a dynamic in which you cannot receive, and in which you reinforce your own fear – thus, you lose. You lose in terms of your own self-image, and in terms of any feelings of satisfaction that you could have ultimately attained. Basically, taking has the same dynamics as indulgence, which also does not allow you to feel satisfied. It does not refresh you, or renew you, or make contact. When we are in a state of independence, we try to hide our taking. We live like ascetics inside, pretending that we need very little. But there is a surreptitious taking.

Look at areas where you may be taking because the subtle guilt that comes from taking does not allow you to enjoy. We take because we do not feel worthy enough to receive. Taking, then, keeps you feeling less than yourself. So in any situation where you catch yourself taking, do what it takes to catch yourself giving.

360 Doubt is a trap you use to stop yourself.

Doubt is one of the best traps of the ego to keep yourself from moving forward and taking the next step. Just at a point where you are ready to move into a higher level of flow or consciousness, doubt assails you. It is one of the ego's best traps.

Many people in a relationship come to a place of doubt. They doubt whether their partner is their true partner, so they go into drought. But you can easily attain a new level of commitment by using the leadership principle and asking yourself, "Who needs my help?" When you respond to that person, your doubt begins to move because doubt is designed to contract you, and to keep you from listening for calls for help. When you reach out to someone, you have naturally set a flow in motion. If you are not able to move through all of the doubt at the moment, you can at least move through a layer of it. Be willing to know doubt is a trap. Do not use it to stop yourself.

If you are doubting your partner, now is the best time to choose them, thereby allowing the relationship to unfold. This is the time your commitment and faith is most needed to move the relationship to a higher level. To know the truth about your partner you would need to see the situation from a progressed viewpoint. This naturally allows you to research your question which doubt has stopped. So today, let go of the doubt and once again, move into the flow.

361 When your heart is breaking, giving creates new birth.

Giving creates a high stage of consciousness and a great deal of love, while heartbreak contracts us and shuts us down.

If, at the point of heartbreak, you take all that feeling moving through you and choose to give with it, your heart and consciousness will begin expanding. At the same time, all the ancillary feelings of despair, futility, uselessness, loneliness, emptiness, and jealously begin to heal – your willingness to keep giving will transform you. Instead of having to go through all the pain of heartbreak, you create an easy birth. So when your heart is breaking, totally give as much as you can because it will save your life, transform the pain, win back the part of your broken heart from the past, and save you a great deal of time that could be lost through heartbreak.

In any situation today, where there is any kind of hurt, just be in service or give through it to find yourself easily moving to a new birth.

Happiness takes no prisoners.

When you feel happy, you naturally feel trust. So there is no reason to control, or to use emotional blackmail to tie people to you. When you feel happy, you feel love and creativity. And when you feel creative, why would you want to control others, or take slaves, or have prisoners? When you take prisoners, you lose a lot of time because you have to be a prison keeper.

In any situation today in which you find that you may be taking prisoners or using emotional blackmail, just allow yourself to choose happiness. Allow yourself to generate the happiness, and as you do, you will move to a level of consciousness in which you would not hold yourself back by taking prisoners.

363

Love is giving everything, while holding on to nothing.

Love does not ask for security. Love just asks to be able to love, to give everything. Nothing can stop your love; it does not matter if the person rejects you or if they run away from you, they cannot stop you from loving them. Love asks for no guarantees, nor does it ask for insurance. Love just wants to love. In that love, is a birthing, a fire that purifies, and the greatness of being. In that love is all vision and purpose in life.

Today, give by letting go. Be willing to let go in any areas where you have looked for insurance, or for some formal way of holding on. Imagine giving yourself totally, as best you can, giving all of you. For when you do, there is no need for control. The love that you give opens you up to a new level of feeling and of joy.

Every failure hides revenge.

When we fail, we are getting back at significant people around us, especially our partner. Every failure in life is also a form of revenge on our parents. So look at all the places where you have failed in your life, and especially where you are failing now. Ask yourself, "Who am I getting revenge on? And what for?" Once you have made out a little list of these particular things, ask yourself, "Am I willing to keep failing in my life just so I can get back at these people?" If we are willing to let all of this go, a way opens for us to succeed.

Revenge and hurt go hand in hand. Where you still feel hurt, you will be getting revenge. All hurt contracts you. Every time you have been hurt you have made your heart smaller. We do this because we somehow feel insulted by what has happened; we feel as if we have been belittled. When we feel hurt or resistant, we are using the situation to make ourselves feel even smaller than we are.

Revenge and failure can continue long after you have forgotten or repressed an old hurt. It is important to find a way to pull ourselves out of the contraction. Any kind of responsiveness will do this, any kind of forgiveness or giving. Many other things create flow, such as appreciation, understanding, trust, integration, letting go, and commitment. They move us out of this stuckness and contraction where our heart freezes, where we lock ourselves into a certain mode of acting – a defensiveness – until we can deal with the pain.

Use your playfulness today as a way of moving beyond any kind of contraction, because play creates flow. Be willing to share anything that needs to be shared, but be playful about that sharing. See how much you can play today, and how much you can get yourself into the flow. Play is the little sister of creativity, so treat it well. It will release old feelings of hurt and revenge if you allow it to do so.

365 "Everybody wants to get to Heaven, but nobody wants to die"

This is the title of a song from a number of years ago. The point is that, whatever Heaven is, it is different from what we are experiencing right now. So to get to Heaven, we would have to change, to die to our present self. We would have to forgive and let this go in order to move to a state of consciousness, joy and love. We would need to reconnect, to remember who we really are.

So what are you waiting for? Get busy right now. Get moving on toward Heaven. Allow to come into your mind the one person that you could forgive, and in forgiving, take a giant leap toward Heaven. As they come into your mind, see what you have not forgiven them for. Ask yourself, "Would I use this to stop myself, or hold it against myself?" Ask for Heaven's help to accomplish the forgiveness so it can be taken care of for you. Your willingness to have it occur gives forth to the situation, moves you forward, and you are free.

Imagine yourself letting go of your present self-concepts that keep you performing all sorts of jobs that do not really belong to you and are wearing you out.

366 God says to us through others, "If you can love me in this form, you can go all the way to Heaven."

The beauty of relationship is, if we can forgive one person about one particular thing, we can forgive all people about this particular thing. So every time we forgive anyone, we forgive everyone. And if we could go all the way to total forgiveness and love with one person, we would find Heaven.

Sometimes we feel much closer to people outside our families than we do our own partner. That is because the person closest to us naturally brings up more of our hidden conflicts. If this same person were further away, we would not get into conflict with them either. But our conflicts help us see what within us needs healing.

See your partner standing in front of you. Look inside them and see God laughing, smiling, and pouring love through your partner to you. Look at your partner and see total love coming to you, wanting to give all of the gifts of the universe. Just receive this bounty and feel how much you are loved. You are loved more than you will ever know.